EMPOWERPRENEURS

Compiled by
Dr. Aikyna Finch

Foreword by
Tameika Isaac Devine

CONTENTS

DEDICATION

To all the people in the world that are making a difference with the businesses or brands they built from the heart!

You are appreciated!!

FOREWORD

By

Tameika Isaac Devine

Everyone knows that October is Breast Cancer Awareness Month. And many of us know October is Domestic Violence Awareness Month, but most people have no idea that October is also Pregnancy and Infant Loss Awareness Month. Did you know that each year, approximately one million pregnancies in the United States end in miscarriage, stillbirth, or the death of the newborn child? Until you or a loved one has been touched by the loss of an infant, it can be hard to believe that 1 in 4 women have experienced the loss of a baby in pregnancy. I know I didn't, until 2014 when my life was permanently altered by the loss of my son during the 37th week of my pregnancy.

The start of 2014 was the happiest period of my life. I had what most people would consider a picture-perfect life. I had an adoring husband that was my best friend, 2 beautiful little girls who brought me joy every day, an amazing career, and I had just started a new business that was taking off beyond my wildest dreams. I was truly living my dream.

A few months into the year, as I was preparing to have some surgery, I learned that I was pregnant. To say I was shocked was an understatement. I was 42 years old and had thought I was done having children. But I was also grateful. Being a mother is one of the greatest blessings of my life, and although I was very happy and content with the 2 precious little girls I had, I knew deep down inside I wanted to have a little boy. And God granted me that desire. My husband and I learned that we were having a third child, and it was a boy.

The next several months, we anxiously anticipated the arrival of our baby boy. We worked on renovating our house, decorated the nursery, purchased furniture, etc. My husband's friends threw him a "Daddy's shower," and my friends threw me the traditional baby shower. We were all ready to welcome our baby.

Since I was over the age of 40, my pregnancy was considered high risk, so during the last 6 weeks of my pregnancy, I began going to the doctor twice a week.

It was a Thursday morning, and I had a doctor's appointment. It started off as any other appointment. As usual, the nurse took me back to get an ultrasound before seeing the doctor. As the nurse moved the probe across my belly, she got very quiet. She asked me when was the last time I felt my baby move. Off the top of my heart, I couldn't quite remember, but I responded, "I feel him all the time." The nurse excused herself to "go get some water" and came back in with the doctor. Next, I heard the words that would change my life forever. She told me that they couldn't "find a heartbeat." My precious baby boy that I was so excited to meet in a couple of weeks was stillborn, and in that instant, I joined the 1 in 4 mothers with babies born into heaven.

In the weeks after I lost my baby, I cut myself off the outside world. Except for my husband, mom, and close family and friends, I did not want to see or talk to anyone. I am an elected official in my community, and as a public figure, it was overwhelming to deal with something so personal publicly, so I shut everyone out.

I started journaling to deal with my grief. My journaling turned into a guest editorial that I wrote for our local paper in recognition of Pregnancy and Infant Loss Awareness Month. After my piece ran in the paper, I heard from so many women who were also 1 in 4 but didn't talk about their loss or their grief. After reading my article, they felt empowered to share their stories and to not grieve in silence. Just because our babies never lived here on earth doesn't make the loss any less than other parents who have lost a child.

This book is a collection of stories from some amazing women (and a man) who have overcome obstacles to get to where they are today. Just as my story empowered other women who had lost a child, the stories in this book will empower you.

DR. AIKYNA FINCH

ABOUT THE FOREWORD AUTHOR

Tameika Isaac Devine is an elected official, attorney and a leading expert and speaker on work-life integration for busy working moms whose insights have been featured in CNN, MSNBC, Forbes, Jet Magazine and more.

As a busy working mom and wife, Tameika understands the challenges that can come with trying to excel both at home and at work. Tameika's personal passion is in helping working moms conquer overwhelm in order to perform their best at work and at home. She is an advocate for women in leadership and speaks on work-life balance/integration, leadership and networking, and politicas and community engagement. Additionally, she has authored multiple books including, "Think Like A CEO, Act Like A Mom: The Pursuit of Work Life Integration" where she shares the perfect blend of sage advice and personal anecdotes to explain how working moms can truly have it all.

First elected in 2002 at the age of 29, Tameika is currently in her 5th term on council and currently in her 3rd year serving as Mayor Pro Tem in Columbia, South Carolina. Tameika is a partner in the law firm of Jabber & Isaac, PA. She is also the Founder of The Possibilities Institute, LLC, a peak performance public speaking, coaching and consulting firm specializing in working with women leaders and working moms.

Tameika's leadership has been recognized nationally. She has been named one of the 50th Most Influential People in the Midlands by Columbia Business Monthly and a 2018 Woman of Influence by the Columbia Regional Business Report. She was selected by Governing Magazine to be one of their 20 leaders in the Women in Government Leadership Program. Tameika also serves as Co-Chair of the National League of Cities' Youth Education and Families Council and as a board member of Women in Municipal Government.

Tameika and her husband Jamie co-host a monthly show entitled with Date Night With The Devines, where they discuss with other high achieving couples love, marriage, raising a family and building success careers.

EMPOWERED TO LEAD

By

Dr. Benedria D. Smith, MBA

Follow The Leader

As a child, one of the most exciting parts of life and play was being the first in just about EVERYTHING. I wasn't the firstborn (no control over that), so I was determined to never be second again. Seriously, I was the first to wake up in the house. I would make my mom's coffee in the morning so it would be waiting on her. I had my school work and daily items ready to go before anyone woke up. You could say as a child, I did more before 6:15 a.m. than most folks did all day. A uniquely organized freak-of-nature child. Semi-early to bed but early to rise. I remember begging my mom to let me stay up just a little bit after 10 p.m. so I could watch Oprah news clips and hear Linda Cavanaugh on Oklahoma's KFOR-TV say: "It's 10 O'clock. Do you know where your children are?" I and my mom would chuckle. She would do the roll call for all five children, and then off to bed I would go.

Back to the first stuff. It is amazing how our natural-born traits shine through before we even realize it. From a child, it seemed my thinking was always forward and out of the box. Call it competitive if you would like, but I look at these behaviors as natural leadership traits that needed to be nurtured. The first thing was seriously an issue for my mom, teachers, counselors, and family. I had it BAD! First to everything. At six years old, I recall my childhood friend Keenya saying, "Dang girl, you are going to do everything FIRST!" I guess my quick nature was apparent to my friends too. It didn't matter if it was to the lunchroom, the playground, or even the restroom break, I HAD to be first! Go figure that one of my favorite games as a child was follow the leader.

In this game, the players line up behind the leader and imitate his or her moves one by one. Players who fail to follow the leader are out of the game. The last player standing is the new leader. In life, personal thinking is that the leader is the last one standing. You know, the "first shall be last and the last shall be first" kind of stuff I read somewhere. I need you to hang in there with me, as I am going somewhere with this leader stuff. So, let's break down the words used in this chapter into some digestible chunks so we are not left with motivational heartburn. I want the words of this journey to ignite those memories in you to find your first and be empowered to take your place in the line of your life.

Leadership Defined

Leadership is defined as the action of leading a group of people or an organization (Oxford, 2019). When you truly look at this definition, being first has nothing to do with being "the ONE" but has everything to do with leading others. Boop! It's not all about you, but it IS so dependent on you being in your rightful position for those who will follow and at one point take their position on the frontline. This is more of a circle-of-life mentality or philosophy of one finding the unique path of life meant just for them and no one else.

First. Being first can be risky. Leaders see what's ahead and inform the ones behind of what is to come. Along with this information comes responsibility, care, integrity, and good judgment. Most will question what leaders see, and that is okay. They are not on the frontline, so your eyes become their eyes, your ears become their ears, and your footsteps set the path to begin new journeys that may not be for you but them. At some point, a new leader emerges.

Once more. Leadership is an action. An action that leads others. So, being first is a big deal and more than an adolescent game. This is real life. But how does one become empowered to lead? Do we choose our path? Some may say yes, but after all I have been through, I say our paths are chosen for us. The only choices we make is how hard or how easy we make it to get there.

Now that we have spoken about what leadership is in a quick scope, let's examine the word empowerment. In this generation, we see it everywhere. It's on billboards, conferences, books, blogs, podcasts, vlogs, and I even mentor teen girls on empowerment each week. The word is ALL over the place, but do we really get it?

Empowerment is the act or action of empowering someone of something: the granting of the power, right, or authority to perform various acts or duties (Merriam-Webster, 2019). So, after reading this, you are probably asking yourself, "When is she going to get to the rest of the story?" I know I would be, so let's go! Being where I am in line was not my choice, but I know that my place in line is purposeful, so that means my life and place has purpose to others. Do you ever feel that way? My hope is that sharing a brief portion of my personal journey leaves you empowered to lead!

So, the last shall be first, and the first last: for many be called, but few chosen (Matthew 20:16).

The Last Shall Be First

I am the giver of useful information. I inspire people. But that almost didn't happen. Almost a decade ago, I attempted suicide. Every day I wanted to die! My dark existed for many years. No longer the eager, energetic girl that was determined to be the "first" in everything; I was last in life. Suffering in silence from major depression, one of the most common mental disorders in the United States. The voices said, "You are not first; you are a waste of space, a burden." I felt so alone.

Fighting for my life. Before my eyes, a series of vivid images of events passed. My mother's face. My dad's hugs. Images of playing with my grandmother's high heels, my first kiss, then my babies … my sweet babies … How can this be changed? Is this the end? Maybe I will be the first in my family to die by my own hands? I remember communicating with God. I told Him "If you take me today, I know I will be with you" because I could feel His presence ALL over me!

In those moments, not sure how long they were, but I remember a promise. I made the promise that if I didn't die, I would take my rightful place back in the front of the line and share His grace and how He spared my life. A life that was to empower others to live. Not just live and breathe but live with vigor and joy!

I had to get to the root cause of my mental illness that was deeply rooted in genetics and life trauma. So, I had to find way back to my place in line, Bee, said I to myself, as I stood in the middle of a dreary time in my life, and comparing the gloom to the days before mental illness changed the trajectory of my life—wherever that was, I knew I had to get better.

To think I thought I was alone. Major depression is one of the most common mental disorders in the United States. For some individuals, major depression can result in severe impairments that interfere with or limit one's ability to carry out major life activities. In 2017, an estimated 11 million U.S. adults aged 18 or older had at least one major depressive episode with severe impairment. This number represented 4.5% of all U.S. adults (NIMH, 2019). Sometimes when you are in the front of the line, you gain knowledge from sheer experience. These experiences make me so grateful for those who have the knowledge to share.

During this time in my life, I didn't rush to the front. I began to go to therapy and listen to other leaders. I would listen to their struggles and how they overcame the battle of the mind concerning mental illness and other mental health conditions. After a few sessions, I began to share my experience. I began to dream again. The little precocious girl was making a comeback! This time, as an advocate for myself. Getting the help I so desperately needed to get back to my family. To get back to life. Could I go back to life as if nothing happened? Like how do you explain being missing from work for 6–8 weeks without having surgery? This required me to do what anyone wanting to rise has to do, and that was, get really clear and really honest about who I was and what I wanted from life before the worse happened. However, I had to go back to my dreams. Plan. Execute it. And live on repeat!

For me, I realized that life is a process, and living a life full of joy is a choice. An attitude of gratitude is a sweet ingredient to complement the savory events of life. I introduce you to the process of Dream. Plan. Execute & Repeat! Yes! Dream. Plan. Execute and Repeat!

Moving on, I couldn't go back. I couldn't give up. No more shackles. The straight jacket was gone, and I was free to move about my purpose. My promise on that dreaded day. Why not? Why not me? I can do this, I thought to myself! I have been a leader from the womb, and leading is about others. I would be a leader in mental health. Shining the light on the dark topics and making the uncomfortable topics comfortable. Keeping my promise and using my gifts to empower others to live with joy.

The First Advocate

Each of our empowerment stories has a unique path from others, but the similarity lies in the definition of the word itself. Think about Malcolm X, the powerful spokesperson for black empowerment who, in 1965, was gunned down at the age of 39 in New York City, continues to influence the political, social, and cultural climate of our society to this very day.

As for or me, I am a living, breathing example that mental illness does not win, but in order to win, we must respect it and care for it like any other disease. Daily, I use my gifts and talents to not only empower myself but also leave a path like Hansel and Gretel—It only took breadcrumb to guide a path for them to find a way home—It only takes us a few steps to guide the path for those who follow our lead—It's like a GPS for joy!

Today, I am a 3-time #1 Bestselling Author, Educator, Filmmaker, Life Coach, and Mental Health Advocate. I use every gift to support talk, growth, community surrounding mental health. It took me a few tuns to get to the right path, but that will happen along your journey.

I spent years reading medical journals, encyclopedias, Edgar Allen Poe, and Hemingway. I spent years looking at maps and studying foreign lands. I spent many nights studying journalists and watching shows and documentaries seeking answers to life's social issues. I suffered and thrived in a mental health facility. I remember the one window my room had. I would look out of it every day to see if a leaf had fallen. I learned to appreciate all seasons of life, good or bad, and know that they ALL work together for my good. I have been cheated, copied, taken advantage of. Through it all, I knew my rightful place in line.

The days of me running to the front of the line was merely a foreshadow of events to come. No matter your place in line, you MUST always know where you truly stand. If you are knocked back, examine where you are. Ask questions. Seek counsel from those in front of you. Ask them what they see. Listen and learn. Be coachable and never stop learning.

If you would have told me even 5 years ago that I would have two short films complete for suicide prevention and mental health, I would have been like … huh? Watching my movie at Harkins Theatre was a dream made reality and ONLY the beginning. Tears filled my eyes because I could feel the shackles and jacket breaking off me. I am FREE! No more chains! No more shackles of self-doubt. No more stigma! I understand my path is bigger than me, and I am just a breadcrumb in the bigger scheme of things. But my crumb is vital to those who battle and will need the stories of how I became empowered to lead even amid adversity.

Today, I am a living product of that promise on the day that should have been my last, but grace! Everything we go through is to truly help others and feel how they feel. All my dreams as a child are a realization of every task. I have traveled to distant lands to share that you can overcome. From Iceland to Cuba, to Australia (and I haven't been there yet), this was a task only complete in my dreams. Sometimes we must go back to the place we were before trauma or anyone told us what we could not be or do. Remember your dreams. Write down your plans. Execute them and be grateful for each day you live to repeat the process!

That little girl that rushed to the front of the line always wanted to be a doctor of the mind, write books, travel the world, and be on TV! Today, that is my reality, and I am empowered to lead others! One day I will be no more, and my time in the sun will begin. I want to lead others to find their place and lead the generations to come

ABOUT THE AUTHOR

Bee Smith is a humanitarian of the 21st Century! She is an International two-time best-selling author, public speaker, mentor, multimedia personality, and mental health advocate. Well known for her dynamic personality and high-impact presentations, she is a tireless community leader, advocate, spokesperson, mentor, and educator. She serves as a local board member for the American Foundation for Suicide Prevention (AFSP), Oklahoma Chapter, and is the creator of the #BeeInspired Digital Brand. Since surviving suicide, she passionately serves local communities and around the world using her experiences as a beacon of hope for those battling depression and mental illness.

Feel free to stay connected with Bee Smith on social media at:

www.beesmith.live
https://www.linkedin.com/in/beeinspired

WHAT MAKES YOU DIFFERENT MAKES A DIFFERENCE

By

Bridgette Wilder

I still remember that day as though it was yesterday. It was August 1972. I was 6 years old and starting first grade … at least that was what I thought. Instead, the school told my parents that I would be placed in special education because they felt, with my epilepsy, that I had "special needs," that I wasn't able to learn like other kids. In essence, in their mind, my epilepsy made me different and not in a positive way.

Fortunately, my parents knew that I was capable of learning. They understood that the medication used to control my epileptic seizures impacted my ability to focus. So, they made a gut decision to follow their instincts. They decided to not put me in special education. Instead, they decided to work with my medical doctors to determine the right dosage that would control my seizures and allow me to concentrate while in class.

Their decision also meant two things that changed the trajectory of my life: 1) I would remain at home for an entire year while my doctors and parents looked for the magical dosage level of Phenobarbital that would balance the extremes of being underdosed and having uncontrolled convulsive body spasms to being overdosed and being a walking zombie; 2) through this experience, I would learn about power. The power of one person to help or hinder another person's life and the power of one's own mind.

Freedom Formula

I had my first seizure when I was 3. My parents told me that my doctors couldn't tell them why I started having them. They just knew that to control the seizures, medication was needed. It was then that the journey to find the magical dosage began. That journey would take four years. Four years of sleeping in between my parents because they worried about me falling out of bed from a seizure; four years of weekly appointments to prick my finger to measure the level of medicine in my system; four years of one little pill that controlled my body, my mind, and my life.

The irony of this control is that this one little pill also gave me the freedom to live life like other kids. So, at the age of 7, I could now go outside without having to wear a helmet for fear I would bust my chin again. I could ride a bike, climb a tree. I could just be a kid.

I was able to start first grade and be with the "regular kids" because my difference didn't consistently stand out. Although I was on medication that kept me from having daily seizures, I still would have random seizures that would come unexpectedly. When a seizure did occur in front of other kids, they would either become afraid of me because they thought they could catch it, or they would feel sorry for me. Needless to say, both reactions saddened me. My dad would wipe away my tears; he told me he loved me just as I was. He told me that although I was different, one day other people would see that difference as special. He told me to believe that what made me different would make a difference to someone else. I didn't understand what he meant back then, but as I grew older, I came to appreciate that being different made me gravitate to those that were different too and innately moved me to help them appreciate the value of those differences.

(Me and my dad, 3 years old, 1969)

The Power Of One To Help Or Hinder

When I returned to school for first grade, my parents were able to get a teacher known for her patience and her ability to help all her kids learn. This infamous teacher was named Mrs. Jones. She told my parents, "Don't worry about Bridgette; your baby is smart, and I'm going to help her." Not only did she help me learn, but she also helped me start to believe that I was smart like other kids. She didn't handle me like I was fragile china. She would call on me in class to answer questions, but she also would set aside time to make sure I understood the lessons. I felt like I belonged. I felt accepted. She saw what I could be and treated me as though I already was.

By the time I was to start fourth grade, the school advised my parents that I was testing well enough to skip fourth grade and be promoted to fifth grade. My parents were excited about my progress but felt that the change would be a hindrance and not a help. They worried that taking me from the friendships that I had developed would be upsetting and impact my sense of belongingness, so they declined the promotion.

The unexpected happened when I turned 12. I stopped having seizures. The doctors monitored me for a while and then told my parents I could be weaned off the medication. So, just as no reason could be provided on why I started having seizures in the first place, there was no reason why I stopped having seizures. What I did know was this: the little pill was no longer part of my daily life. I no longer needed it to be normal. I was normal on my own.

The Power Of My Own Mind

I can't explain it but knowing that I didn't have to take medicine every day gave me newfound freedom. Freedom to just be a person and not just a condition to be figured out. But like all freedoms, there was an unspoken price. I didn't have seizures, but I did have body spasms that would occur when I became overly stressed or if I continuously held my emotions in. I soon realized that to control my body, I had to learn to control my mind and express my emotions.

I started paying attention to the signs that a body spasm was going to occur. For me, that meant my left arm would start with a mild tingle that would progress to a painful twinge. Within 10–20 minutes, I would have a body spasm.

Knowing the signs helped me control my mind. I learned that if I could concentrate on something else, I could control it long enough to get home so that I could release the body spasm. To some reading this, it may sound impossible and improbable. But to a pre-teen girl that experienced the trauma of judgment from others viewing it, learning to control her thoughts was not an optional life skill; it was a survival skill. A skill that I utilized until I was 30. By this time, I was a ninja at mind control. Instead of minutes, I could control it for hours, which was needed because I was working full time. If I felt the signs, in addition to focusing my thoughts, I would go to the office fridge and get my secret weapon—popsicles. For some odd reason, the cold from the popsicles helped to calm me down and then get

Zen in my thoughts. That's hilarious, but it worked. I was able to finish work and go home. Once there, I would have body spasms for most of the night, get up the next day, and start the process again. Fortunately, I learned over the years to incorporate exercise, a healthy diet, and journaling my thoughts to balance my stress and manage emotions.

The Road to Empowerment & Entrepreneurship

At 22, I started my career at the community college that I got my degree. I was hired by the Career Center that I visited several times a week to begin my job search for the "elusive first job" that all college grads seek. I went so often that I began to have friendly chats with the Center Director, Patricia Lloyd. I was a Computer Science major and she was impressed by my knowledge of computers and my initiative in looking for a job. She hired me to automate the Career Services Office, but it evolved into something greater. She not only gave me my first adult job; she also became the north star that led me to see my uniqueness as a gift to help others.

When Patricia walked into a room, you felt her presence. She had a bohemian style coupled with a smile that lit the room and a personality that made you feel as though you were talking to an old friend, even though you just met. She owned who she was. She was comfortable in her skin, yet she also gave you the freedom to do the same. I had never met anyone like her but knew deep down that she would change my life, and she did.

While working with Patricia, she taught me business and people skills. Although I had no experience, she assigned me projects to manage job fairs and help students find jobs. She told me she had confidence in me. I didn't want to let her down, so I gave 110% to exceed what she asked me to do. I grew so confident that I started my first business, Communications Link. I taught technical skills, created resumes, and did career coaching. Patricia had her own side business as well and, in fact, hired me as a subcontractor for a contract she had to teach keyboarding.

Although I was Patricia's assistant, she treated me as a business partner. She would discuss her vision and goals for the office, incorporate my input, and encouraged me to do more to get to the next level. She didn't want me to limit myself. Like Mrs. Jones, she saw what I could be and treated me as though I already was. She saw greatness in me even when I didn't see it myself. She was honest when she saw that I wasn't ready to move on to a new role, but she also helped me to see my differences as a gift that can mutually benefit me and others. When I was ready, she gave me her blessings because she knew that the wounded bird that flew into her nest was now ready to take flight and experience the world. She was a friend then, and 30 years later, I'm proud to say she still is.

Through my work with Patricia, I realized my hidden talent of working with people and got my first exposure to Human Resources. You see, I majored in Computer Science because I didn't want to work with people. Mainly because of my negative experiences growing up of being judged because of my seizures. I found technical people were more my vibe because everything was more about the bottom line. It wasn't about whether they liked me; it was about what I produced. Working with Patricia, I learned to take my analytical and big-picture thinking that I learned from my technical background and apply it to working with people. My strength was that I could be objective and neutral when hearing people's problems. Because I was introverted, I was a good listener. My challenging life experiences because of my differences allowed me to have empathy when listening to employee or applicant concerns. I, the techie that didn't want to work with people, found out that what made me different also gave me a unique power to help others.

From Techie to Human

Although I realized that I was good at working with people, I did what many people do. I didn't pursue it. Instead, I pursued my initial dream to become a programmer. I got a job as a Software Automation Specialist with a bank. I excelled at it so much that my manager told me she wanted me to train the people in the bank on how to use the software that I programmed because she thought I would be good at training others given my background from the college. Two years had passed since that time, and my reflex was to say, "No, I'm a programmer, not a trainer." My manager politely said, "Well, you have to." At that point, I decided I needed to build on my people skills, so I went back to college to major in Human Resources. I kid you not; from the first class, I realized that was what I was meant to do. So, I graduated and pursued an HR career. I also started HR consulting and helped my clients solve their individual and business challenges.

My career was going well so I put my consulting business on hold until life smacked me in the face and reminded me of my calling. My job was eliminated, and I was a divorced single mom with bills to pay. Necessity begets action, so I started my consulting business again, and Wilder HR Management & EEO Consulting was born to provide customized HR and EEO solutions to small- to mid-size businesses. I decided to narrow my niche because I wanted to help businesses that like me, wanted to make a difference for the clients that they serve, yet, given their size, didn't have the resources to have a full-time HR function. I wanted to make a difference that would matter to the existence of their business.

As I reflect on my life's journey thus far, I have had many highs and lows both personally and professionally. I have lived a life beyond what I ever imagined. I have fought battles that I did not always win. Through it all, I always come back to the words of my father: "Although you are different, one day other people will see that difference as special … what makes you different will make a difference to someone else." You know what? He was right.

ABOUT THE AUTHOR

From HR Manager to Chief Human Resources Officer, Bridgette has created fundamental human resource policies; developed training programs in Diversity, Ethics, Leadership, and Workforce Management; and brought stability and structure to organizations. She has worked in both the private and public sectors, inclusive of such industries as transportation, telecommunications, business services, city government, higher education, non-profit, and banking. Additionally, she has experience working with union, non-union, and service contract (SCA) employees.

Bridgette is the owner and principal consultant of Wilder HR Management & EEO Consulting, which focuses on simplifying HR for small to mid-sized businesses through customized solutions to manage their HR function.

Bridgette's most recent role was with the City of Memphis, where she served in the dual roles of Equity, Diversity, Inclusion & Safety Officer, and Senior Manager—HRBP. She was responsible for the operational and strategic management of diversity and inclusion, workplace safety, employee relations, labor relations, OJI, drug testing, corporate social responsibility, civil service, HR Business Partners, unemployment administration, policy administration/ development, and federal/state compliance. Additionally, she led and collaborated with HR Centers of Excellence and divisional leadership on organizational change management initiatives related to total rewards, talent management, training, and performance management.

Prior to her role in the City of Memphis, Bridgette was the Chief Human Resources Officer for Media Fusion. During her tenure, she established the Human Resources Department and was responsible for the strategic and operational areas of talent acquisition, employee relations, compliance/risk management, benefits, diversity outreach, and compensation analysis. Additionally, Bridgette was the Human Resources Manager at the Verizon Wireless Huntsville Call Center. She had strategic and operational responsibilities in the areas of employee relations, benefits, compensation, and staffing. She also was responsible for ensuring consistency in the administration of HR policies and practices.

Bridgette's other work experience also includes holding positions as Deputy Director of Human Resources/Chief Diversity at The Citadel, Military College of South Carolina. She was the first African American Deputy Director and the only person to hold the dual role: an Employee Relations Representative & Corporate Trainer for Airborne Express; Manager of Recruitment & Training at INROADS, Inc. in Richmond, VA.; Market Source Corporation where she marketed IBM personal systems to the VA higher educational system; Automation Specialist for SouthTrust Corporation and Jefferson State Community College where she coordinated job fairs, presented career seminars, and provided job assistance to undergraduates and alumni; and Communications Link which she owned and specialized in facilitating career planning and software training workshops.

Bridgette earned an MBA from Averett University, a BA in Human Resources from Birmingham-Southern College, a BS in Workforce Education from Southern Illinois University, and AAS in Computer Science from Jefferson State Community College. She is a graduate of the Diversity Leadership Academy and a recipient of the Coretta Scott King Humanitarian Award. Bridgette's awards include the 2013 Verizon Wireless Customer Service Leadership Award, 2013 Verizon Wireless Modeling the Credo Award, and 2012 Black Achievers Corporate Executive Award.

Bridgette is a member of the Forbes Human Resources Council and the SHRM Expertise Panel for Ethics & Corporate Social Responsibility.

Feel free to stay connected with Bridgette Wilder on social media at:

https://www.wilderhreeo.com
https://www.linkedin.com/in/bridgettewilderphr

TAKE THE LEAP

By

Vanessa Canteberry

Many of us have a story we would like to share and maybe put into a book form, but the majority leave it as only a thought—I used to be one of them. Often times I found myself writing, and eventually, my thought would turn into a poem. Poems that allowed me to express my frustration in a story form, as opposed to me screaming at the top of my lungs to the person who hurt me again, only to fall on deaf ears.

Being a loner and an introvert, I don't open up much for many reasons, and when I do, I eventually would be let down again. It happened quite a lot; I would keep things bottled up to the point I was ready to explode. So, when I found my outlet in writing, it stayed with me, even up to this day. It's painless because I no longer have to explain myself to be left unheard again. However, in this paper, I can read it out loud, and my energy will begin to shift.

Growing up in a toxic environment, you tend to pick up that behavior, and I wanted to be able to find a better way of expression. Though uncertain how to go about it, I was willing to take the leap to find out.

The best thing that I could ever do was to begin following my dreams and goals, no matter what someone thought of my vision. I've overcome so many things and challenges in my life, and I know there are so many other people going through it. With me sharing my story about how I was able to overcome so many things in my life and how I was able to make it better, it only made sense for me to accept the fact that I was going to expose myself to the world by sharing my story.

Too often we will give an excuse as to why we choose not to move forward and share our truth. It could be family; it could be friends; it could be our minds; it could be the generations that we had seen before us—they did not move forward, neither did they share in our goals, dreams, and aspirations. So, it only makes sense for me to give another excuse to add to the list to not share my story.

I also realize that I felt a different way when the ink hit the paper, and then I was able to read back my thoughts. I was able to react differently; I was able to manifest a better version of myself, but I never thought I would write a book that would lead to writing more books by taking that leap. And that leap started after I was laid off in 2011—when nobody would hire me regardless of my 20 years of experience. I did something different. I created an experience and opportunity—or better yet, a business—that many needed, and I just didn't know that it would be this big. 2013 was when it all began—researching, investing with my unemployment check before I ran out, with my teen children in the background, rooting me on. I experienced many losses from those people whom I thought had my back, long-time friends that I considered to be family. Even the family that I considered would be there no longer existed. So, I accepted the fact that it was me and my children on this journey of what to become, with me taking this leap. I took that leap; it wasn't easy. I tumbled; I failed; I procrastinated; fear showed up, and even the naysayers thought I would never be able to do the impossible. I did it anyway. With much prayer, I moved forward, and I didn't look back, no matter how many times I wanted to throw in the towel. I was at a point of no return.

2016 became my reality of me becoming a self-published author. Not only a self-published author, but I also became a best-selling author. My business is now being known because I did the impossible, and so many people want to know how they, too, can be able to publish their book. I just did not want to only publish my book; I wanted to do something that the publishing companies weren't doing—teach you how to turn your book into something more. So, I was on a mission to educate people about how they, too, can self-publish their books and turn them into something else besides just becoming the best author. I've learned lessons from speaking to many publishers, one of which is how they really, truly take advantage of the vulnerability of individuals who wanted to become an author, not showing them how they could tap into the marketplace by doing what they have grown to love.

Being creative with my business, I was doing something different that I knew was needed but unheard of … but I did it anyway by taking that leap. I did it for me because I was told I couldn't, and I refused to listen to the naysayers.

Never in my wildest dreams would I have thought that I would self-publish eight books within three years. The demand for me to help other people self-publish their book is at an all-time high; it even attracted a celebrity client through someone who had reached out to me years back and always remembered our conversation and connection.

So, share your story. Build relationships. Being authentic and loving what you do is a blessing in disguise. I said at the very beginning that I wanted to write and share my story in a book. I never wanted or had any intentions of helping others to write their book, but being obedient would stretch you. At the end of the day, it can cost you but will pay off.

I'm a believer that books open up doors, but again, you have to be willing to write the story in order for the book to become a reality. My books have touched so many lives around the world, and when I hear the feedback and how much it really open them up in knowing they are not alone, I know I am on the right path. This goes without saying that my book turned into books; it allowed me to become a speaker, a mindset coach, a book consultant, and now I'm preparing for my second annual conference.

I'm grateful that I was able to go through the healing process of my journey prior to writing my stories, which are now in books. I no longer have to worry about what somebody thinks or says about me as I share my story. I do know that my story is unique, so no matter what anyone has to say, what I have written in the books is my truth. And my truth is healing one household at a time. So, don't worry about what others may think about your story. It will only prevent you from sharing it because you never know who is waiting on you to share your story, but you have to be willing to write it.

There is no better feeling than seeing your clients who had held onto their book finally take the leap to move forward, and now they are being booked to speak and are selling out their books.

The client who was referred to me was told by a publishing company that she needed to pay $35,000 in order for them to help her publish her book. Not only did she get her book self-published with us, but she also returned to start the second phase of turning her book into a monetized business.

I am often contacted by individuals who had spent money on publishing companies only to get abandoned. They finally need our services to help them complete the project.

The biggest test was to move forward by helping first-time authors become authors in an anthology series in which I again did not want to be part of for many reasons. One is that I never wanted anyone to feel the way I felt when I was involved in a similar project which ended up becoming a huge mess. A mess where I had to remove myself in order to move forward in the vision that was given to me—to self-publish my own book.

Unfortunately, sometimes we want to bypass the process and get to the purpose and end up having to restart and go back to the basics. The basics are the ground work they would attempt to avoid in order to get to the first step. But to get to the first step, sometimes you need to take baby steps and/or even crawl. Still, in all, remember, it's a process, and it takes time.

Do not focus on the success of others in order to determine how successful you will become. You don't know what it took for them to get there, and most are not transparent in sharing the good, bad, and ugly moments of being an entrepreneur, let alone a successful one.

I say this to you: be empowered to explore the possibilities of doing what you are called to do.

Fast forward, being an entrepreneur is not easy, but being laid off was a blessing in disguise that I never knew, but now I understand. I had a bigger mission besides sitting behind a desk, limiting my gifts. The company that laid me off in 2011; it's the same building I walked back into in 2019 to meet my celebrity client for the very first time. So, imagine if I didn't take the leap, if I continued to procrastinate, continued to allow fear to show up, continued to make excuses, continued to listen to what naysayers had to say, or continued to just sit in self-pity. I would not be walking in my gift and owning my purpose.

Your story is somebody else's survival kit. Share your story.

ABOUT THE AUTHOR

Vanessa Canteberry is the CEO of InspiredByVanessa. She was born and raised in Chicago, Illinois. She's determined to continue to break the cycle of poverty, negligence, and unnecessary hardship. Vanessa worked in Corporate America for 20 years as a secretary. After being laid off in 2011, she knew something needed to change, knowing she was a single parent of three. Vanessa was not able to obtain employment, and the mere thought of being unable to support her son attending high school and two daughters attending college was unbearable.

For that reason, Vanessa challenged herself. She took a stand on faith and changed her mindset. She's on a mission to educate individuals on the importance of transformation of the W2 mindset in life and business.

Vanessa is also the business owner of Breaking Barriers Unapologetically and a co-host of Motivate Social Podcast. She is a speaker, mindset coach, self-published 7-time best-selling author, and she works from the comfort of her home. She is also committed to teaching individuals how they, too, can become business owners and overcome obstacles in their lives.

Your past does not determine your destiny; make what seems impossible possible. InspiredByVanessa stands on

FAITH and refuses to allow FEAR to void VISIONS that need to be seen and heard on so many platforms. Vanessa teaches you that you are more than a W2. She is the best-selling author of Shifting Your Mindset and Breaking the Cycle of Brokenness, co-author of I Am More Than, and Do I Not Matter? She is also the compiler for the anthologies Screams of a broken woman and cries of a broken man and Dear Dad and Dear Mom. You are not alone in your journey!

Feel free to stay connected with Vanessa Canteberry on social media at:

www.Facebook.com/InspireVanessa
www.Linkedin.com/in/vanessacanteberry
www.Instgram.com/InspiredByVanessa
hello@InspiredByVanessa.com

I KNOW WHAT THE WORLD IS MISSING: MY GREATEST ME

By

Dr. Pamela Caldwell

I tell my students that before you can understand anything, you have to know the story, the back story, how it came about, how it started. I am going to take my own advice and tell you how it started. My Greatest Me: Becoming, Being Sustaining (MGM: BBS).

The beginning started with a social media post and pictures: (see below). Please note, I did change the post; I had to delete some information where others were tagged.

Left, March 31, 2016, and Right, June 9, 2016

"I do have a story behind this journey ... and it wasn't just one thing; it was a combination of things over the years. The final straw was when I looked at my goals and the legacy I wanted to leave, and I looked in the mirror, and I had to be honest that I wasn't going to have that legacy if I didn't change my physical body. I couldn't live with the thought that I wouldn't be able to help others become great because I decided not to be my greatest. The journey began. I started with what I had in my diet and becoming aware of why I ate what I ate and the damage it was doing internally. Also, I found (changed sentence to take out brand name) this weight management product that worked for me. Those two things have been the biggest change. Have I hit the gym? Not yet ... May 18, 2016, was the last day I wore the walking boot which I had been in since October 2015. First, I had to learn to walk again. It is better, but I still have days where it hurts to walk. I do strengthen exercises at home, and I know that one day I will be able to go to the gym and incorporate the exercise part. I must admit I have been on this journey many times, but this time, I am enjoying the journey. I am doing this for me in order to help others. Until next Time, Just Know That I Am Becoming My Greatest Me ...."

At that moment, I didn't realize that the last statement "Becoming My Greatest Me" would become the idea for my business. I further enhanced the tag line when I thought well what happens when we complete the Becoming stage: do we just stop, or do we keep going? That's when I thought of

Being, the stage of living and enjoying the progress and process. Then I was thinking well what happens after Being: how do we pass this knowledge on to others? How do we Sustain? This is how the concept of "My Greatest Me: Becoming, Being, Sustaining" started. This concept is what we use at The KAM Group to help individuals navigate transitions. The idea started with my weight loss journey; however, I soon learned that this strategy can be used for any transition that I wanted to achieve. In this chapter, I will explain the concept "My Greatest Me: Becoming, Being, Sustaining," giving an illustration of how I used this concept when I received an opportunity to teach Business in China.

Explanation of My Greatest Me

I recall when I was writing the post; I said that I needed something catchy, a tag line. It took me a moment to come up with something. However, Becoming My Greatest Me was what I came up with. I can't say where it came from; it just popped into my head. I wanted something that was personal so that when people would say it, it would be personal, it would be for them, created for them by them. It would become their personal lifestyle that only they could control and say when it would start, end, and how it would continue. I am a believer that we need more personal stuff and understanding how our unique self fits into this world. We need a space where if you are not what society refers to as "typical," it's okay; there is still a place for you. We need a space for that one that may feel they don't fit. I am here to say that we don't have to follow the norms; we don't have to fit. We just must Be Our Greatest Self; we must be our authentic self. When we are our greatest self, our authentic self, that is when we can transition into finding our place in this world. This is the place where we learn that we do not have to be like someone else. Why? Because the world already has that someone. This is the place where we learn that what the world is missing is My Greatest Me.

How do we develop this lifestyle of living My Greatest Me. A lifestyle that not only for ourselves to live, but also living in a way to pass this way of thinking to the next generation.

A framework of living in order for us to leave this world a little better, also to teach the next generation how to be better, do more, in order for them to leave this world a better place than it was when they arrive? How do we transition into this lifestyle of My Greatest Me (MGM)? By Becoming, Being, Sustaining (BBS).

Explanation of Becoming

Becoming - the process of coming to be something, the process of preparation (Webster's Dictionary).

The coming to be something is coming to be My Greatest Me (MGM). The Becoming stage, also what I refer to as the Preparation stage. The stage where you prepare, let go, and embrace. Prepare your mind, body, and energy. You let go of the past, and you embrace the future.

To demonstrate this concept, I will use my story of moving abroad.

Becoming Illustration

I never thought about living outside of the United States. Traveling? Yes, but living? Nope, never. I could not see myself living that far from my parents, where I could not drive to see them or, if they called, drop everything and go and be there within 10 hours, and that is if I drove. However, 2016 proved me wrong. This was the start of me Becoming. You recall how I started this chapter with the picture? Well, I didn't know that Becoming My Greatest Me would help me with this new experience.

I was looking for employment because my full-time job ended because the educational program I was with ended. I was looking for virtual work because I wanted to venture into entrepreneurship. I kept filling out applications, and one day I saw an ad for a Business Professor for a US school but for their location in China. I didn't want the job. It was just about applying for jobs, and this one, I didn't have to fill out the long application. I only had to email my information. I did, and I've been there since February 2017.

I must admit that once I hit send, I forgot about it. Like I said earlier, it wasn't like I wanted the job; I was qualified, so I applied. A few days later, I received an email saying they wanted to interview me. I was like: "OK; I need the practice." I was interviewed. I asked at the end, "So what is the next step?" He said, "I will review with my boss. If we decide to move forward, we will send you a contract." A few days later, I received the contract. The process, from applying to signing the contract, was short; the process of becoming an expat took a little longer.

Prior to the interview, I thought it was a good time to prepare my parents, but first I had to prepare my mind. I had to decide and play the what-if game. What if they offered me the job, what would I do? I thought about it and decided I would at least try it because who knows where it would lead to? After I decided that, then it was time to tell my parents. I remember when I told my mom; she was like, "What? Talk to your daddy." Then I told my dad; he was playing that selective hearing game, but when I said that it was a US school; however, it wasn't at their location there but in China, he got really quiet. He chuckled and then said, "Well, will you be okay with it?" And I said, "Yes, Dad, I will be okay with it." Then he said, "Then I will be okay with it. However, your mom and me aint coming that far; we are too old for that." My mom was like, "Your daddy doesn't know what he is talking about." Needless to say, my mom was still hesitant. However, she accepted that I wanted to do this and wished me well.

This was a part of me preparing my mind. Once I made up my mind, it didn't matter what people said, and people did say things, but I had already prepared my mind to take the adventure, and it was: "No talking me out of it!" Even when my dad became ill, had surgery, and shortly passed away, I still decided to go.

As I mentioned earlier, I had already begun preparing my body when I decided to take my health more seriously and how this concept came to life. It was when I made this decision, I began to look at my diet. What was I really eating? Once I became aware of the food I was consuming, I had a benchmark to work from. From here, I made the decision about what would I add to my diet that was healthier, that would push out the bad stuff. I know this may not be the way most of us, and I included, in the past would start the transition of weight loss. However, this time, I wanted to be more positive, so I started adding healthier stuff; then I didn't have room for the bad. One of the first things I did was to add more water. I started drinking 1 gallon of water each day. Let me tell you; I had to become very creative in order to complete this goal. Once I added the water, it naturally decreased my soda intake.

Preparing my energy. I had to decide how I was going to experience this adventure. Was I going to experience China, or was I going to only look at how China was not like the U.S.? I decided I wanted to experience China. I had to prepare the energy that I was giving out into the world and that I would let into my inner circle. I arrived in Changchun on February 15, 2017, about 6 weeks after we had funeralized our dad. I was grieving, and I was starting something new. I had to decide how I was going to become an expat and grieve. I decided it would start with me and my energy. What was I going to give out and what was I going to accept? I knew I was grieving, but I didn't want everyone else to know. I wanted to grieve my way and in my own time. I also understood that my defenses were down, and I needed to protect what energy I released and took into my inner circle. I had to be self-aware to the extent of knowing when it was time to just let myself grieve and when it was time to experience this adventure. I had to learn that it was okay not to be okay some days. One thing I refused was to let my grieving be a reason for me to be bitter and not experience what God had created in China.

After I began preparing my mind, body, and energy, I had to "Let Go." I had to let go of the idea of where I thought I was going, where I thought I should be, and where I saw my future self. I had to "Let Go" of the idea of the plan that I had created, and I had to embrace what this adventure could bring into my future.

This is Becoming.

Explanation of Being

Being - the nature or essence of a person (Webster's Dictionary).

Being is the second stage of the B-B-S Concept (Becoming, Being, Sustaining). This is the stage where the Becoming is lived. The stage where your preparation is part of your lifestyle. I feel this is the stage that a lot of us miss when trying to achieve our goals. We forget to live; we just want to prepare and sustain.

Let me continue with my story of moving to China.

Being Illustration

As I stated earlier, being is the living stage, where one gets to live what they have become. I prepared my mind, body, and energy. I let go and embraced my future. Now it was time for me to Be.

I moved to Changchun on February 15, 2017. I did not speak any Mandarin. I had only talked to the Dean via video Skype, and I had a picture of the lady that was picking me up from the airport. I was living by faith. When I landed in Beijing was the time I started to Be. I was being an expat. This was when I had my first situation; I missed my flight to Changchun. I had to recall my Becoming stage and use what I had prepared in order to get on another flight, contact my job, and let them know I would be late. I did it and made it to Changchun.

For almost 3 years, I have been an expat. I have been living abroad. Yes, it has been an experience and adventure. Sometimes it has been scary and so hard. When it becomes scary and hard, I go back and revisit the Becoming stage. When I return, I must prepare my mind, body, and energy; I must let go and embrace again. When returning to the Becoming stage, I had to renew my mind, body, and energy. By renewing, I mean, I had to remember the reason behind this assignment. Renewing my body might mean I had to rest. Renewing my energy, I had to evaluate the energy that I had been giving out and accepting in my inner world.

Living abroad, I finally feel I am able to Be My Greatest

Me. You see, I was always the one that wanted to be the best, at the top. I soon realized I didn't have to be that. What I had to be was MGM. When I am MGM, then I would be my best; I would be at my top. This was something that I learned in the Being stage. Before, I was trying to be someone else's best, at someone else's top, and I was never going to get there and be there because that wasn't My Greatest Me.

This is Being.

Sustaining

Sustaining - providing physical or mental strength or support for self and others (Webster's Dictionary).

Sustaining is the stage where you not only provide mental and physical strength for yourself but the stage where you pass it on as well. MGM is also about teaching others about this concept. How are you sustaining Your Greatest Me? How are you passing the concept of "My Greatest Me: Becoming, Being, Sustaining" on to the next person, to the next generation?

Sustaining Illustration

How am I passing this idea of MGM: BBS onto the next generation? I am not just passing it on to a generation in the US; I am doing it globally. I am a Business Professor, and I teach many management courses. You see, when I teach management, I always start with self and tell my students that management is about knowing and living your authentic, your greatest me life. I teach this concept when teaching management and other business classes. I tell them it starts with self and understanding how self fits into the world.

When people ask me about China, I tell them from my perspective of living here. When I meet people through social media thinking about living abroad, I share my experience and give them the good, the bad, and the ugly about living abroad. I share my idea of MGM and the BBS concept. I live my message of navigating transitions.

This is Sustaining.

Conclusion

I have given a brief overview of My Greatest Me: Becoming, Being, Sustaining. I discussed the different stages: becoming, being, sustaining. What you must know is that these are not stages that you pass through once to get through your transitions. It is more of a cycle that one can use to navigate their changes, their goals. As people, we usually do not have just one goal that we are working on but several, and usually, we don't have one completed and then move on. We have several that may be going on all at the same time. MGM: BBS is a cycle where you may be in one stage for one change, but in another for another. Then you may have to revisit a cycle in order to move forward in order to continue this path of My Greatest Me: Becoming, Being, Sustaining.

ABOUT THE AUTHOR

Dr. Pamela Kay Caldwell is a transitional coach, and owner of The KAM Group, LLC. Dr. Caldwell started The KAM Group when she decided to use the skills of teaching and coaching used in the classroom to start a business. The KAM Group helps individuals navigate life's transitions using the framework "My Greatest Me: Becoming, Being, Sustaining. At, The KAM Group we believe that in order to navigate transitions successfully first one has to identify their greatest me. Once this is identified then the person can create a plan of how to become, be and sustain it.

Dr. Pamela K. Caldwell is an educator and author. She received a Doctorate in Management with a concentration in Social/Environmental Sustainability and an Executive MBA from Colorado Technical University. She also received a Bachelor of Science in Civil Technology, Construction Management from University of Houston. Dr. Caldwell was born and raised in Dover, Oklahoma, and also has lived in Texas, Dallas and Houston. Currently, she resides in Changchun, China, Jilin Providence. Dr. Caldwell is a Business Professor at Jilin University Lambton College, a higher education institute that partners with several schools located in the United States and Canada. Dr. Caldwell teaches Undergraduate and Graduate courses in the areas of accounting, business management, leadership, environmental science, and project management.

Dr. Caldwell is a co-author in the anthology Dear Mom, and will be a solo author in two upcoming books.

Feel free to stay connected with Dr. Pamela Caldwell on social media at:

FB Page: www.Facebook.com/TheKAMGroupLLC
FB Group: www.Facebook.com/groups/MyGreatestMe
Instagram: www.Instagram.com/kam.group
LinkedIn: www.linkedin.com/company/the-kam-group
Website: www.thekamgroup.org

GETTING TO THE OTHER SIDE OF HAPPY

By

Tresa Simmons

How do you feel when you love someone who doesn't feel the same way? I decided to ask my mind, body, soul, and spirit.

You see
I thought it was the outside world that had forgotten me
But, Noooo
It was I
Emotionally immature
Bankrupt
Keeping Score
Zero, zero, zero
Corrupt
Hijacking my own sanity and peace
Disgracing my space
Telling my body it's too …
You name it

I did not want to claim it …
My beauty
My own reflection …
My greatness
As I fought for my own limitation
My spirit grounded
Too heavy to fly
Carrying tears
Of a grieved Soul
Loving me who could not love her back

"Getting to the Other Side of Happy" was a phrase that would pop into my mind at will for several years. I had no knowledge of what those words really meant, although I would use them in a mantra periodically. I had no idea the phrase did not refer to a destination but a life-long commitment I held internally, unconsciously, about my freedom. A freedom that requires of me following my inner wisdom and the coordination of dancing with the wildest parts of myself which, at the core, is really about my connection with my unique brand of authenticity.

As in all things, life unfolds. When it does, more often than not, our unfolding happens in increments, leading us back to ourselves the parts of us that tried to love us, but for various reasons, we rejected our own self-love. I toned down my brilliance, criticized my body, stopped listening to my deepest desires, and turned away from my inner guidance system—my intuition—in search of what I thought was outside of me, only to return home to myself. The path to getting to the other side of happy taught me that happiness is what comes to me in the form of delight or pleasure by outside stimuli. Joy, on the other hand, is the ability to embody and generate contentment, pleasure, and delight from within. The first is based on one's surroundings, and we are at the mercy of our feelings, depending on what emotion is elicited. In the second, the response to life is not determined by emotional whims.

Like most children, I have longed to be happy since I was a small child. In fact, the journey of getting to the other side of happy likely began at my birth. It has been an extremely rocky road. My mother graciously passed down the oral history of my childhood, as well as hers, and told the story of how poor her family was in rural North Carolina. My mom's poverty-stricken childhood life was difficult and may have prompted her to accept my father's proposal. She married him when she was in the eleventh grade—at the tender age of 17. Although she planned on finishing high school early on, this goal would evade her for many years. Instead, she did what many women did during that time. She bore four children and focused her life on her family.

I was the second eldest child. According to my mother, I cried for six months. Then suddenly the crying stopped. Over the next several years, I became an extremely solitary child. During my formative years, I barely spoke. In fact, I did not interact with my peers very much until I was about six years old, right around the time I started first grade. I preferred my own company over my siblings, cousins, or anyone else.

I remember overhearing my paternal grandmother say during that time in my life "something is wrong with that child." It was in my mid-40s that she explained she did not mean there was something 'wrong with me,' but it was not normal for a child to sit in silence hours upon hours. I recognize now that I had internalized her words to mean either I was a bad person, not good enough, or something was odd about me. In hindsight, I see I was in a deep state of meditation, and my spiritual sojourn began at conception.

For as long as I can remember, I was searching for validation of my existence and my right to have a seat at the table of life. I searched for a connection to my inherent power and love as something I did not possess but was waiting for it to be handed to me. Who knew, because I did not, that I was seeking more of myself? However, I sought Goddess in others as a way to feel complete and fulfilled. I looked in religion, used spiritual bypassing as a way not to do my inner work but appear if I had, took class after class, and I had the expectations that if only the man would act right or if other people would do right, I would be happy. I played small, toned down my light, stuffed my emotions, and changed the cadence of my voice or voided it out to be accepted, never understanding what I was doing was futile and a mission that could not be successfully carried out.

I see it now you holding on like a door on its last hinge
Crying, screaming, and raging yes at them, but at me
I see you, said you, after all these men took like on a drunken binge

They kept coming back for more all the while I was
screaming for you to see my ability to restore
We were broken pieces torn apart from greed and lust of
what was not theirs to have
But I was there to help you to abort the pain
However, your mindset in agreement with them had
become one of self-abuse as you said let it rain
You did not deserve this treatment, and I was trying to
free us both as we were like one bird with two broken
wings
I finally understand Maya's poem; I know why the caged
bird sings
I was your younger self walking on broken glass
And you, my friend, were the worst kicking your own ass
Your pain would not allow you to see you had a friend in
me
Today, we merge victorious me strong and at rest
experiencing peace at its best
No more crying, not just for what I saw you go through,
but also because you now understand I was there for you
You were never alone, and I took care of you … as best I
could … like a shoe that was too little for your feet trying
to take on a role I was definitely unequipped to meet
I love you, but I like you more
The woman you have grown into no longer needs to keep
score
Instead, you have merged with your younger self me, and
we are happy
No more living from broken pieces

Now living our lives in the roots of wholeness
Being restored and remade in Spiritual Boldness
I would not change nothing for my journey, although I
did not feel that way then
Happier times are upon us because you took time to help
me see within
I am your younger self. I am you.
I see you
the strength you embody is you
the epitome of power
Power in all stages and phases of a mental shift from
brokenness to "I am the shit; don't fuck with me. I am a
bad bitch."
As your younger self, I get to take a seat, enjoy my place
while you reign supreme, making no apology for taking up
space
We did not understand that to gather all of the scattered
pieces was part of the plan
What did I know? I was as immature as I was young, but I
held on tight to those pieces like a door on its last hinge
Unable to stop men from taking on their sexual binge
The last laugh is ours, a gift of our strength unknown …
at the time
A powerful merge of our younger and older souls
Unfolding as
The gathering of our pieces is our story now being told

Life happens as we often hear, and it happened to me. It
changed my internal narrative from joy to fear. My

childhood was riddled with struggle and pain. My siblings and I witnessed domestic violence in our home. One day my dad jumped on my mother and beat her severely. When my mother saw he pulled clunks of her hair out, she blacked out from the pain and rage and lost control. She scalded my father with hot water. I still remember the screams. Although that was the end of the beatings, my parents did not separate right away. I later saw many repeated patterns of my mother and my father in my own life. My father was emotionally unavailable to my mother and his children. He did not provide financial security nor safety for my mother, which I think she thought she would have with him when she moved from home with her 9 siblings and mother.

My mother and father divorced after 10 years of marriage. She eventually remarried, and she and her new husband moved our new family to Michigan right after Christmas in 1972. He left all of our things between Virginia and Michigan, saying that our car could not pull the small U-Haul. The reality is, we would not have had a place for our things. I later learned my stepfather had been living with another woman before relocating our family to Detroit. On December 29, 1972, two days before the New Year and 17 days before I turned 11, my mom and stepfather exited at I-75 and stopped at a rest stop off Gratiot Avenue. It was extremely cold and harsh weather … a prelude for life as my siblings and I knew it.

My welcome to Michigan had a hint of the trouble coming. After sending my mother and siblings, including his daughter, to eat, my stepfather sat me on his lap and started rubbing my vagina mainly stimulating my clitoris. That was my first initiation with a man. It's funny what one remembers, but I remember it felt good. Nevertheless, I did not tell my mother nor did not allow him to touch me again. The repercussions that came from me saying no were often cruel and unusual punishment. This was the beginning of a cycle of sexual abuse that would come from other men molesting me and sexually abusing me. The colorful dreams of my childhood turned black and white with airplanes always falling out of the sky and scenes of the ocean raging and in turmoil. My mind began to protect me.

I know my mom loved her children and took great care of us as best as she could. But she, too, was wounded, felt abandoned, and disillusioned in a distant land, trying to make her second marriage with a man who did not have the same intentions ... a man I saw for several years go between his mistresses and my mom ... a man who I watched bring his early 20 something-year-old lover and their newborn son in our home with my mom standing in the middle of them, holding the baby. The mistress stood boldly in our home as if she owned it with no remorse. I think I knew something was wrong. I had stopped trusting myself, and the numbing had begun. In retrospect, I can imagine my mom cried out of our presence from this humiliating experience.

By the time, I was in high school; I tried to commit suicide in the 9th grade. I can see now I did not want to die. Who dies of hyperthermia? To this day, my feet are sensitive to the cold. In the 10th grade, I met a young lady in an after-school Bible study group. She later became my sister-in-law. I have a better idea of how gangs form, as I became close with her family and relatives. There were quite a few of us around the same age. It came a time I had to choose my spirituality or choose the group. I chose the group to meet my need for physical, emotional, and mental touch. This decision became one of many I made that closed the door on my inherent voice and innate wisdom. Every decision I made that went against my convictions eroded my faith in myself. I submitted to my fears of being abandoned and alone, a story that I subconsciously nursed for many years.

This created a belief that justified the lie that I was not enough, not good enough, and I could not be responsible for my life. I eventually married my children's father from a place of dire emotional neediness. I had convinced myself that I needed someone to boss me around, and he carried his own pain and needed someone to boss around. After divorcing him at 6 ½ years of marriage, I remarried him. When we do not learn our lessons, they repeat. We divorced after almost 10 years later, and those years were, in many ways, a repeat of my own childhood drama. Through it all, I never totally turned my back on my relationship with God as I knew her. But I learned to carry guilt and shame like a heavy tumor on my back … in my bones. I had become adept at literally gathering pain into a ball in my mouth and swallowing it. I felt the pain as it slid down my esophagus before I would pick myself up and pretend all was well.

In 2016, my call to return home (inward) became louder, yet I had no clue this was what was happening to me. I returned to therapy after attending for several years on and off. This time, with a new therapist who was not interested in me retelling my wounding story. She was about supporting me in becoming self-empowered. She did not discount what happened to me, but she turned me in the direction to see I was not as helpless as the story I was telling.

I started seeing myself differently. It wasn't 'an outsider' that became my salvation, although I thought it would be. Journaling about my feelings of being abandoned and my feelings attached to that idea led me to see I always had me. I was the gift to myself that I had not cultivated because I was too busy looking outside of myself. I have always had the gifts of clairvoyance, clairaudience, clairsentience, and Clair cognizance that guided me and help navigate when I listened.

There are many examples where my intuition has shown up. Here are a few: First—I recall a really vivid moment of how my clairvoyance manifested in my childhood. When I was a 13-year-old child, I saw a casket on my bedroom wall. Shortly thereafter, my mom received a call saying my maternal grandmother had passed. There was another time my mom received a call saying my sister had been taken by her child's father from our father's home in North Carolina. My siblings and I were residing in Michigan. I began to pray. I had a vision of her walking into my bedroom, and within 2 weeks, she did.

I knew the moment I finished having sex at age 17 that I was pregnant. Some call it intuition. Others call it reading energy. Nine months later, I gave birth to my eldest. I attended a retreat a couple of years ago. Before going, I dreamed of trees that I have a connection with. When I got there, I was standing in the middle of the trees that appeared in my dream. The opening in the trees to the sky was the exact image I saw.

Someone broke into our home when my son was a couple of months old. I was speaking to my sister who lived next door. My son began to whine, and he rarely cried. I thought to myself, He must be hungry. I had a habit of turning all of the lights off in the house, except where I was. As I went to get my son a bottle in the dark, I never saw but felt a presence. At that moment, I was able to read the energy of the intruder. I later was told that there were two men in the home. After notifying my sister and her boyfriend that someone was in the house, they brought their dogs over. One intruder ran out the front door, and one ran out the back door.

WHAT WOULD I BE WITHOUT THE JUDGMENT?

Answer: I AM
I AM …
Light and free
Poetry in motion with....
No rhyme or reason

Happiness, joy, peace, love wrapped in laughter
Bowing down to my own significance
Authentic
Beauty in the vortex
Colors and energy of bright reds, oranges, greens, yellows,
pinks, blues
Nurtured by my own breast
Healing words and flowers

I AM
The power of self-pleasure in real time
A climax of passion in my daily life called Tresa
Entering into a praise of energetic vibration
Connection of heart
A salutation
Humble
Thankful
Gratitude is my Strength
Powerful
Playing in space that has no time

I AM
The call of the Siren for the Feminine Divine
The vortex of my womb that meets my Yoni in Yes

I AM
The sun and the moon in motion lighting my way
Singing in cacophony with the rain and the thunder
The rainbow and the wind

The trees and the seed
I AM
More than enough
A statement of my greatness

I AM
Brilliant
Phenomenal
Ancestors beating the drum
I AM Uniquely ME

It was also in 2016 that I took a process called the Juicy Womanhood Rites of Passage. This was when I learned that I had been living my life through the lenses of pain and struggle. I was not living authentically. I was still carrying my grandmother's words: "something is wrong with that child." I saw how it had shadowed my life, from not wanting to show up for myself to burying my gifts so as not to appear different, to marrying someone who I thought was more equipped to take care of me, to the lies of not being enough or good enough. I carried my biological parents' and stepfather's pain. I carried the pain of abandoning myself. I carried the pain of subjecting my own children to what I had gone through. I vowed to bring a new native tongue to my lineage. A language that fully dispels intergenerational suffering. I cried, journaled, prayed, meditated, and struggled with blame, shame, and depression as I wrestled with letting go of helpless Tresa. After all, that, too, had its payoff.

At the end of the rites of passage was a consecration. The

guest informed my sisters and me that the story we tell, we get to live. One of the most powerful takeaways for me was: broken people (women) create more broken people (women). The first statement hit home right away, and the second statement did not fully register until my entrepreneurial voyage. I learned that everywhere I go, there I am. For every way that I had not done my work, it was showing up in currency, whether that currency was money, people, time, etc., or lack of those things.

I used to think the rites of passage meant I had somehow arrived because I knew I had been changed. What really happened was I took an honest look at what I called life and saw I was existing and existing in a cloak of bottomless hurt. The kind of hurt that was so profound it motivated and undermined every decision I made. I committed to moving the needle from empty, struggle, and pain to pleasure and oneness with my body. The inner work had just begun, and my commitment became the down payment that no matter what, I would follow through. A year later, I began feeling traces of depression, I thought. But I was grieving the loss of the only identity I knew. Two years after going through my grieving process, I understand how what I have coined Deception Deficiencies can undermine our progress and make us believe we 'are good' or 'we in a good place' when in actuality there are levels to our healing.

I found that old habits can be challenging to release. Seeking outside validation is still one of my challenges, even with having coaches, a therapist, mentors, big sisters, and friends that support my growth. They call me out when I forget my value or forget I'm the prize in the relationship or when I fall into old patterns of numbing out. Wanting to take my life back in an active way, I started a book club in February 2017. Community Conversations with Meaningful Dialogue lasted about 6 months. I knew that I was not the only woman on the planet particularly my age that felt like a late bloomer and or a woman who just wanted a different life but was not sure how to go about getting it. It was my thought that we would read different books and support each other. My first book was Women Who Ran With the Wolves by Colette Estes.

After the book club did not pan out, I started a Facebook group. Conversations with a Sister is the voice of women of all of ages and have been in existence about a year and a half. This was a great place to have discussions with my sisters. Yet, I knew I had more to offer in the way of supporting us in a greater capacity. I know that people perish for the lack of knowledge … and … for not utilizing said knowledge. I also know that many of us had no idea how to activate the knowledge we were learning. I felt called to be transparent about all that I had gone through. It is my hope that my story of pain, struggle, and abuse becomes a story of possibility and triumph. The stronger my voice became, the louder it became. I felt compelled to answer my invitation from the Universe.

Conversations with a Sister: Healing One Conversation at a Time was born in June 2018. I would host the show on the

Zoom platform and invite co-hosts to share the topic at hand with me. No topics are off limit that uplift and educate women. This level of healing opened me up to coaching. The Pleasure Coach is such an appropriate title. My life was shifting as I knew it. I started my business The Womb Space: Healing Nature's Way and filed the paperwork with the State of Michigan. On October 22, 2018, I became an LLC business owner. I took the Womb Sauna Certification class and completed it in November 2019.

In the interim of me completing my certification, on March 14, 2019, VOICES took her first breath. VOICES stands for Voicing Our Integrity Choices and Expectations Successfully. It is a sacred space, aka the CIRCLE, which meets bi-weekly. Women come together with facilitators known as spiritual midwives, be they man or woman in the CIRCLE. The spiritual midwives educate and engage the sisters present while helping them become the best version of themselves. Some of the topics covered in the Circle have been about self-care and health (coochie care, women are more than mothers, the benefits of breast massage and ovarian breathing, and other forms of breathwork); relationship topics {breaking struggle love cycles, healing womb trauma); sacred sexuality topics (the healing power of orgasms, self-exploration, the miss-education of sexuality, sexual healing; Energy healing (the chakras, astrology); and the Divine Feminine (the identity of a Goddess, Goddess worship is our birthright, codes for Goddesses to be the architect of their own reality).

I, like Dorothy of the Wizard of Oz, had to learn I was already home. I am proud to be an empowerpreneur. I did not earn this title when I started my business. I began to express the qualities of what I had no words for and began to personify said qualities. As I embraced this aspect of myself, the nature of an empowerpreneur expressed itself through me as my soul's work. I found myself:

- Accepting more graciously my leadership role and owning all of my experiences.
- Accepting I can't save the world. I can only save myself, and it is my hope that I leave enough clues that teach women the answer is inside of themselves.
- Reprogramming my mind.
- Seeing the gift and the value of my own company.
- Understanding my rage is just as sacred as my anger.
- Admitting emotions are my superpowers and my north star.
- Seeking out support from my tribe of sisters.
- Utilizing my therapist, mentors, and coaches.
- Remembering all life experiences are gifts in the form of lessons.
- Seeing myself and my clients as powerful beings who are not their wounds.
- Articulating my signature creativity.
- Allowing the expression of my humanity by living deeply from my heart space.

- Telling myself and others the truth around the hard and somewhat embarrassing stuff.
- Facing my inner child is still a priority for me, particularly around feeling abandoned and validated.
- Knowing theory does not produce lasting change, but embodying it creates space for change.
- Forgiving myself, which is self-love in the form of tenderness.

Getting to the other side of happy is the joyful energy that I carry into what I am being and what I do. I am not an empowerpreneur because I have it all together. I am an empowerpreneur because I stand in my yes to a vision to be of service that is larger than me. I tackle social justice issues that impact women in my distinctive way and talk about uncomfortable topics. I am an empowerpreneur who is on the planet at this time to amplify the Divine Feminine energy in a holistic way while offering the gift of authenticity, healing, transformation, wisdom, magic, and compassion fused in love in the work I do.

As an empowerpreneur, I refuse to be defined by my back story or deny the power of my pain story to resurrect me. My past is just that—my past. But my future is being written every day. I am mindful that the woman I am today will meet the future misses. I want both to be proud of each other. Self-love is my gift to me as my womb continues to hold my dreams. My account of how I got to the other side of happy is my gift to every woman. May you find your voice, gather the courage to listen to her, and the wisdom to ride her wings to that heavenly place of joy.

ABOUT THE AUTHOR

Tresa Simmons is the CEO and founder of The Womb Space: Healing Nature's Way. She has been on a spiritual journey from her mother's womb and in her latter years became more accepting of it.

Due to trauma having its origin in her childhood, Tresa suffered with poor self-image and poor self-esteem that lasted well into her adult years. However, it has been that same trauma that supported her in birthing the woman she is today.

In 2016, Tresa went through a rites of passage program which she says helped her to connect deeper with the desires of her heart and soul. It took a couple of years before she was able to decipher the language of her soul.

Tresa is a holistic health and wellness practitioner and entrepreneur. Her love is womb wellness, sacred sexuality, and energy work. She identifies her nature as that of a High Priestess of the Divine Feminine. Tresa says that she has been called a witch, a rootworker, a tree hugger, Womb Goddess, and a medicine woman by others. She calls herself a Womb Whisperer and the Pleasure Coach. According to Tresa, Somatic healing is very important for women to make a connection with their bodies.

Tresa compares herself to a strong tree that is rooted in her purpose to support women in getting to the root of their issues by journeying inward and reconnecting with their womb and to support women in shifting their soul legacy.

Her branches are the Conversations with a Sister Series, the Legacies Unleashed: Healing Generational Suffering, and VOICES (a virtual birthing circle).

Tresa is a visionary, life coach, author, speaker, and poet. She is a Usui Reiki I practitioner and a certified Womb practitioner through the Womb Sauna University. Tresa is a lifelong learner who says that she will continue to further her education that supports her core passion to empower women who are on their healing journey.

Tresa likes to read and exercise, particularly to run; spend time with her 9 grandchildren, family, friends, and with her sisterhood tribe. She has a secret desire to learn to belly- and pole-dance.

Feel free to stay connected with Teresa Simmons on social media at:

https://www.facebook.com/tresa.simmons
uniquelybrilliant2@gmail.com

YOU MATTER

by

D'Adriewne Pickett

Throughout our journey, from season to season, there should be a time where we re-examine where we are to see if we are where we want to be. Seeing what works, what could be altered or changed to become a better version of ourselves. I believe that everyone looks back at their life, wondering if there were a different life that they should have had. Was I truly born for this life? When I was younger, I had that thought: Was this the life I was supposed to be living? I wondered if I was delivered to the wrong family. I felt out of place. I did not believe I belonged there. Have you ever thought: What if there were two of me, living the life that I need versus the one I want? Have you ever come to the point that you are not an island to yourself, and you cannot do it on your own? Now you realize that you have some work to be done, and it is a personal journey, and it is an inside-out job. It is a personal and day-by-day job; it is time to get real with yourself. Have you ever been in a position where you felt that you were out of control, and where you imagined you would be was not where you found yourself? The people you thought that would be there were not there. There will times when things will be out of your power of control. There will be things that hurt you intentionally as well as unintentionally.

You feel your life is not your life anymore. You place people above your own needs. You feel alone, and no one is there for you when you need them. You feel you are doing everything alone and have no support.

Your Job experience …

There is a story in the Bible of a man named Job. He had his life turned upside down, and his life changed. He lost his family, money, etc. His friends came against him; they thought he did something wrong and started questioning everything that he did. What they did not know was that it was his time of testing, and he was building his testimony, and neither did he. He did not know that his enemy went to God for permission to test him on purpose, and God said, "Have you tried Job?"

In your journey, have you had that Job moment where, no matter what you did, things kept coming against you, your life changed, and everything was out of your power of control? You felt like you had nothing and no one; just your faith and trust in God. I have heard that you must fall to know where you stand. This is the point where all you have is your faith in your Higher being just to make it. You have fallen, and the only way up is knowing you cannot do it by yourself; you need your Savior.

My Job experience…

A change … May 16, 2018, I was on my way to pain management for a sciatic nerve, and I fell and hurt my knee. I ended up in the hospital, had surgery, and went to my first rehab facility, which was not the best place. The first day, I fell out of bed. They overdosed me; they did not do their job. I was upset because I, too, was unable to do my job. After two more surgeries, I left there. Thus, after three weeks in the hospital, I went to my second facility, which was better but still had issues. I was released to go home on August 12, and on the 13th, I was back in the hospital because I had fallen again. After the fourth surgery, I went back home to try it again. After a while, I realized that I needed more help than I had thought. I stayed with a few people, which brings me to this point in my journey.

In the end of July 2019, I had the wonderful opportunity to spend some time with my grandma. I watched her every day get up, worship, read her word, listen to a sermon. What a legacy I have come from. I went there because I heard God tell me, "I want to take you to the place where you first fell in love with Me. A place where you decided that you wanted a relationship with Me." Growing up, I went to church whether my mom sent us or not, and I went with friends and/or family. At the age of 13, I went to an apostolic church. There, we tarried for the Holy Spirit, and I received it but was not told what to do next. I wanted to live right for God but did not know what that meant. At the age of 16, I had my first child. At the age of 19, I moved to Montgomery, where I met God. For a while, we were having an up-and-down relationship. Now we have a relationship that I know I love Him, and I cannot live or breathe without Him.

The Seed

There has been a time when people went before you, saw something more in you, dropped a nugget of seeds on the inside of you and let you know that you are more than what you see. The first seed that we have is our conception. The Bible states that God knew us before we were ever born. He designed us before were even thought of. He gave us the parents that birthed us; although growing up, we may have felt that it didn't work for us.

Truth Moments

Growing up, I thought I was born into the wrong family or someone swapped me. I felted unloved and unwanted. However, I had to learn that people can only give what they have, and to have something different, you need to do something different. Even though people want a change, sometimes you try and give up or don't know how, and your environment speaks louder than the change.

I know my mom and dad loved me and gave what they

could, and what we did not receive, I believe God sent people across our path to assist us in going forward. I remember my third-grade teacher picking me up, taking me to church, and making me a part of her family. When I went to the next grade, she let the teacher know that if she had any problems with me, she was down the hall. Then there was Ms. Brown that picked us up and took us to camp as well as different community programs showing the love of Christ, teaching us crafts, and spending time with us at her home as well.

My mom sent us to church and made it possible for us to be a part of different experiences. I went to an apostolic church, where I learned to tarry for the Holy Spirit with the evidence of speaking in tongues. I wanted to live right, but my environment spoke louder, and no one taught us what to do next; they just said, "Don't do it." At age 15, my school counselor challenged me to write a ten-year plan of what I wanted to do in life. At the age of 16, I started having children, and then I started being talked about over the pulpit, and I just stopped going.

Before I moved to Alabama to go to school, there was a guy I was dating at the time. His name was Christopher, aka "Butch." He asked me why I hung with the type of people I did because I was nothing like them; another seed sown. Throughout our journey, I believe there will be people to assist us to get to the next level.

The Watering

Once a seed has been planted, sometimes we get it right away; however, there are times that things must take time to develop. A time of processing, where it can be rooted in you, and it becomes a part of you. You need to come to a point where you become instrumental to the growth of other people, where you become your own client and realize you need to live by what you profess.

I shared some information with a friend of mine. She took it and rolled with it. She came back and told me, "Thank you; you made me a lot of money." I see a lot of people take my information, work with it, and advance in their journey, being who they were created to be on purpose. It's the watering.

I am starting to think that we all need to water the seeds that were planted in our lives. There is a scripture in the Bible which states that we were meant to love people as ourselves. The problem is, we do not see ourselves as valuable, neither do we believe in ourselves as much as we do other people around us. Have you come to the point where you matter? How do you see yourself? How are you investing in you? Are you watering the seeds that God has planted in you? Are you being all that you were you created to be? Take the time to think about these questions: Where are you now? Who are you now?

It's OK to learn from other people, grow from them, but you need to be in the game for yourself, believing in yourself. You should be your biggest cheerleader; you should be showing up for yourself; fighting for you; watering your dreams, visions that God has placed on the inside of you since the day you were born. You were created for a purpose. Are you living what you were created for? Are you intentionally living all that God designed you for to its fullest? Are you showing up for you on purpose? Are you loving you intentionally, unapologetically living on the purpose that you matter and were called to live the life God created you for? Are you there for you in the good, bad, and the ugly? Every decision, thought, action, are all a part of the journey. It all works together for you to be the best you always, if you choose to use it for the positive.

The Fruit

Throughout our life's journey, we will have the seed that has been imparted in our life since before our conception. There's One who fashioned us before we were ever thought of. We were designed, created for a purpose. We did not have control over who we were born to, but I do believe it was for a reason. The seed that was planted in us; there were people who came along to give us what we needed in the season that we needed it in. We learned lesson intentionally or unintentional, through our hurts, pain, joy, or blessing, and then we grew from there. It is in the watering stage we start believing in ourselves, realizing that we matter just as much as the people we love and take care of. We start believing and investing in our goals and dreams on purpose;

intentionally, unapologetically living on purpose, showing up and fighting for us.

In the fruit season, our eyes are open; we take responsibility for the part that we play in our journey. In all, the good, bad, and ugly work together, and it is all we have become. We get to learn as well as grow daily. This is a daily journey and it is personal we get to decide the life that we want to live. Sometimes we get things right, and some days we don't. It is said that 80 percent is what happens to us; 20 percent has to do with how we respond or react. We have choices, even when things are out of our power of control. Nothing or no one is perfect, but we can strive to be the best version of ourselves daily. There is no right or wrong way to live, we make decisions based on our choices that we have. We do what we feel that is best for us in a season of our lives and hopefully, we get it right; if not, we get another opportunity to readjust, learn something new, and try again. It is said that an unexamined life is not worth living. I believe that we get to look back to see what works and what doesn't and determine what to do next.

Life is what you make it. You get to decide your purpose and, of course, your journey.

What is Next?

This is our journey. We get to decide what is next in this season of our life. We have our goal, but what are some steps to get you where you want to be?

You've got to decree and live on purpose.

Example: I will live the life I was called to live intentionally, on purpose, being my biggest cheerleader.

It's said that you love people the way you love yourself. How do you love yourself?

Example: I am beautiful and loved by me. I matter!!!

You will be what you see ...

Put a picture of what you see and write it down. Allow it to become a part of who you are on purpose. You matter!!!

The Prayer

"Father, thank You for not giving up on me, for giving me a purpose and a destiny. Thank You for teaching me to show up and believe in me. Without You, there will be no me."

Write your own prayer and decree you are worth the fight.

ABOUT THE AUTHOR

D'Adriewne Pickett is the founder of Re-Inventing Yourself Consultation, where she counsels, mentors, and coaches others in their change process within a wide range of ages. D'Adriewne has worked with clients from 5 years of age and older. Her specialty is working with families, women, and children. She works with them to overcome life issues that they are experiencing in that moment, taking the negative and seeing the positive possibilities in life. D'Adriewne assists them to realize their value and worth; it is not about what has happened but how to take that information and make it work for them, resulting in a positive outcome. She empowers each person she encounters to gain a greater understanding of their part to play in their personal journey. She assists them in seeing their side and taking responsibility on their part, whether positive or negative. D'Adriewne works with individuals in the six stages of change. She assists them in seeing change as a process and a personal journey—it begins with the individual and what is in their power of control. D'Adriewne assists them in understanding that things may have been done out of their power of control, but they have control over how they react or respond. She inspires those she works with to do the personal work in their transformation. Change for everyone is different, although the problem, solution, and techniques are different based on the peculiar need of the person. D'Adriewne embraces both traditional and non-traditional forms of counseling, such as aroma in therapy, music in therapy, energy release, drama, and play in therapy. D'Adriewne assists clients to realize that this is a personal journey, and it's a day-to-day adventure in discovering who they are and the legacy they want to leave behind.

Feel free to stay connected with D'Adriewne on social media at:

https://www.facebook.com/dadriewne
gdstldo@gmail.com

THE PATH TO GREATNESS: YOUNG MAN'S JOURNEY TO BECOMING

By

Dr. Larry D. Parker Jr.

As a young black male from the Eastside of Temple, TX, I never thought I'd be in a position to be sharing empowerment stories with others. In school, I always performed well but was labeled by teachers as "too busy," or my mother would often receive a report that I was "talking too much." As a single mother for my early childhood, she was never happy to receive these calls. Thankfully, these labels and behavioral observations did not limit future teachers from seeing something in me as early as my mid-elementary school years.

Many people would not think that being raised, predominantly, by a single mother would result in one's ability to thrive and be placed in gifted classes at a young age. We were fortunate enough to have the support of elders in my family and community to support us. Much of my time outside of school was spent with my paternal grandmother and great-grandmother. From them, I realize I gained a great deal of wisdom and emotional strength. They taught me about respect, perseverance, and humility as observed in their ability to sustain family life with very little means. They did not make excuses for limitations or areas of lack and always held onto their faith.

When I think of my first experience of what it means to feel empowered, I recall the Star Fire Program. This was a program that consisted of gifted children that were bussed to a magnet school from other parts of the community. This particular magnet program removed all limits on education and fostered cultural exploration. As I entered the Star Fire program in the third grade, I would be a part of a program that exposed me to an educational experience without constraints that I was not accustomed to, to include foreign languages, orchestra, and education. It was not uncommon to be performing significantly above grade level in the program which left less room to be deemed a mere "busy body."

I see now that my elementary school teachers were ambassadors to the world beyond our neighborhood, which was empowering to my foundational years. Many of my teachers within the Star Fire program came from communities far from mine. At an early age, I saw that education was a gateway to experiences beyond my local environment, and it was because my educators believed in me that I was able to embark upon this journey. I had the great fortune to be exposed to a diverse representation of educators that would provide me an academic foundation beyond the binding of a textbook.

It was because of this foundation at home and in my early school years that I was able to then thrive in the college and military settings. I developed a keen sense of developing relationships with individuals that were knowledgeable and willing to be positive influences in my development. At the same time, I also learned how important it was to identify situations and persons that were not aligned with my goals. Although not the easiest thing to do, knowing who to keep in and out of my social and professional circle.

As I look back on my career within the military and as an educator, I think of all my encounters with amazing people and cultures around the world and how it empowered me. I spent years of my life in Asia, North America, South America, Australia, and the Middle East. I worked close enough with individuals to become familiar with their individual work ethics and their personal values. Although the cultures were extremely different with regard to the food, and clothing, the one constant that I noted was that the people that I perceived as successful and influential were grounded in strong values such as respect, humility, and perseverance. I saw over and over again the foundation that my grandparents set for me was a universal approach to success.

The one thing for certain that I could count on as a leader within the Marine Corps was a career full of dynamic experiences and challenges every day. There were never two days exactly the same. There were never any situations that could be perfectly planned. My military experience provided me with countless opportunities to employ, hone, and test my values and leadership.

In total, I completed 24 years of active duty within the United States Marine Corps. Along the way, I had the great fortune to pursue both my professional and personal education. It took the better part of 15 years to complete my master's in business administration and doctorate. I overcame the challenges of family responsibilities, active duty, and combat deployments. I have taught college courses for over 10 years. Contributing to the body of knowledge that has helped me throughout the years.

As I recall my professional experiences and contributions to others along the way, nothing compared to the joy felt from the positive influences I had on others. First and foremost, it was rewarding to know I was there for my family when they needed me. Second, it was good to see the positive level of influence I had on others by imparting some of the wisdom I gained along the way in what I called "mentoring moments."

Once you begin to think about empowering moments in your life, many significant instances that were major decision points in your life come to mind. Instances that

you could have chosen to give up or take the easier path to less success.

When I look at my life thus far, I see how each situation

or challenge was a building block to the next. The important thing about empowerment was to recognize it for what it was; an opportunity to do better and be better. That opportunity required personal accountability.

I purposely saved the point of personal accountability to the end. I can recall on several occasions throughout my life being asked to identify the source of my positive outlook and perseverance. Lacking any real thoughtful response, I would respond with a simplistic answer: "This is just how I was made." Upon reflection, I know the answer I gave was only partially correct. In addition to the positive role models and positive environments that you may be blessed to have in your life, there must be a level of personal accountability to be successful.

Success is defined as different things to many people. I achieved a number of great things throughout my life. It is genuinely humbling to look back on where I started to my position in life now. Adversity to someone only accustomed to success will test that person in ways they may not have been prepared. It is in those times of self-doubt, fatigue, and stress that you must measure your passion and purpose for your goal against the cost. Are you willing to pay the cost, and is your purpose for doing it in the first place greater than the trials you go through along the way?

I was fortunate to learn the lesson that hard work could pay off early in life so that as I began to encounter problems, I knew there was a success on the other side of hard work. I just had to keep moving and staying true to the process.

A person can be provided with advice, opportunity, and resources, but that person receiving has to put it all to use. In instances a challenge is encountered, the drive to push through the problem comes from within. I believe hard work and discipline to the proven process will get you through adversity along the path to your goals.

The passion for the purpose has to be a fire that can be stoked from within. That is likely the one aspect about my environment I can't give any more of a concrete answer. I believe in God, and feel I was blessed with the ability to recognize the blessing of opportunity. I woke each day with the intent of not wasting a chance to be better and pursue the best in life. The writing of this book provided me an opportunity to acknowledge many of the supportive and invaluable persons in my life. The details are in the book.

I will close by quoting a sign I recently read, "Education is the most power we can use to change the world." The pursuit of my education assisted in empowering me and making a positive change in the world. I am pleased to share my story of empowerment with the release of my two books: *Manage the Circle* and *The Path to Greatness*. *Manage the circle* is a more in-depth discussion of the principles of personal accountability for your environment and network. *The Path to Greatness* is the story of my journey that may serve to inspire anyone that can glean lessons from how I overcame my challenges.

ABOUT THE AUTHOR

Dr. Larry D. Parker Jr. currently serves as Contributing Faculty, Doctor of Business Administration Chair, Walden University. In this position, Dr. Parker mentors doctoral candidates that are researching solutions to complex, real-world business problems. Through research and mentorship, his students build advanced decision-making skills. Dr. Parker is Adjunct Faculty, ADEN University, and teaches two courses: Leading a Global Team and Personal and Managerial Leadership. It is within the construct of these courses that Dr. Parker teaches skills that facilitate successful leadership in a dynamic global business environment.

In addition to his service as an educator, Dr. Parker is a Lieutenant Colonel in the United States Marine Corps and currently serves as Command Inspector General (CIG), Marine Corps Forces Central Command (MARCENT) at MacDill AFB, Tampa, FL. Commissioned in the Marine Corps in 1995, upon graduation from The Basic School (TBS), Dr. Parker was designated a Supply Officer. His career includes a myriad of logistics leadership assignments in the United States, Asia, and the Middle East. His Headquarters Marine Corps (HQMC) assignment was within the Equal Opportunity and Diversity Branch. At HQMC, Dr. Parker served as a program manager for diversity outreach to community influencers and college students. Dr. Parker coordinated Marine Corps Leadership Seminars at universities throughout the United States to share his personal experiences and leadership training.

Dr. Parker is a graduate of the following professional military education: The Basic School, Marine Corps Command and Staff College, Joint Forces Staff College, Defense Equal Opportunity Management Institute (DEOMI), Air War College, and Department of Defense Inspector General (IG) Course.

Dr. Parker holds a Ph.D. in Organization and Management from Capella University, a Masters of Business Administration from Liberty University, and a B.A. in History from Wittenberg University. His published research is a qualitative study of the experience of organization members within the Leader-Member Exchange (LMX) Theory "out-group" of their racially different immediate supervisors. He is a member of the Association of Inspectors General.

In addition to being a proud father of two teenage sons, Dr. Parker is a lifelong entrepreneur on various scales. In 2014, Dr. Parker leveraged over 20 years of business, logistics, and supply chain management experience to launch P42 Trucking LLC, which is a subcontracted trucking company operating throughout the southern gulf-coast region of the United States.

Feel free to stay connected with Dr. Larry Parker on social media at:

https://p42consulting.com
https://www.linkedin.com/in/drlarryparkerjr

QUEEN GET YO LIFE BACK

By

Cheryl Guidry

Who asks for a divorce with two kids in college and two in high school and after being accepted into graduate school? I mean, who does that? Me! This queen did just that and was thrust into a season of discovery. After 21 years of marriage and raising a family, I had to figure out who the hell I was and who I was becoming! I was the queen who took her role as wife and mother seriously. Everything I did had that purpose in mind.

From undergraduate school to a master's degree and all the work and certifications achieved between, I was living out my goals. I wanted it all; a loving family, autonomy in my career, and the flexibility to enjoy the second phase of my life. Two decades and a year gone by, I came to the realization that I failed to do my work before committing to a relationship where higher education and entrepreneurship were not mutually in the plan. Heck, we didn't have a life plan! There was no discussion at all about critical life matters; no deep dialogue about each other's vision and purpose, no premarital counseling, and no love language work before I DO. There was more of an emotional need and a physical attraction which was superficial and fizzled out with each blow to the marital foundation caused by family challenges. So, in a place where I did not recognize myself as a queen anymore, the real work was beginning. I had to put my big girl panties on and deal with the death of a relationship. I vowed never to marry again, and if I did, it would have to be by divine intervention.

My story is common for many busy entrepreneurial queens. She is superwoman, successful and confident, able to leap from a corporate meeting to a PTA meeting in three-inch heels in a single bound. She works hard at her craft. Starbucks is her morning boost and many times her only source of nutrition at the start of the day. She can state her vision statement in 30 seconds with a smile and ultra-confidence. When she walks into the room, she is noticed, hair and nails, clothing; she is well put together. But her heart has been broken, and her loving spirit severely wounded. She is Queen Superwoman until the pains of a failed marriage or a relationship takes over in those quiet moments when no one is looking.

Can you relate? If so, you likely asked the same big question I did. How do you get your life back after it has been turned upside down because of a failed relationship? You probably also have a lot of inner and girlfriend chats around these thoughts. *How did I get here in the first place?* How do you motivate yourself to start anew in a relationship? *How can I keep from hiding, by focusing on career goals? Will I detach from my desires for an abundant life with a significant other?* Living fully and loving again is a challenge many successful queens experience as they push past the pain of divorce, being widowed, or dealing with choosing the same jerks repeatedly.

Many Queens hide behind the masks of pseudo-happiness, successful businesses, sorority affiliation, church and community involvement yet remain broken. They juggle corporate meetings, podcasts, speaking on stages and hold their ground in the courtroom without missing a beat, but they lack success in the love department. Love seems evasive because they are also masking past wounds by clocking numerous busy hours. The queen hiding from love makes no time on the calendars to focus on self. With responsibilities like children or perhaps caring for elderly parents, added to limited or no work-life balance, this cycle of masking continues. The longer the mask-wearing lasts, the easier it is for the subconscious mind to convince my sister queens that they are happily single. Others continuously attempt to seek out new relationships before allowing the wounds of their past to be healed. Many times, settling for relationships that do not serve them.

Let me introduce you to three of the queens I had the pleasure of working with and the various types of baggage they carried. (The names have been changed.) The first I will call **Queen Charlotte**; she is a divorcee. Twelve years into her marriage, infidelity reared its ugly head. The man she gave her life to and had three beautiful children with cheated not once but twice. He vowed after his first breach of trust never to do it again, but less than a year later, there was a new other woman. She was done! Charlotte recalls, "He had the nerve to want yet another chance. Not no, but Hell no, would he put my health in jeopardy again!" Even with that, Queen Charlotte expressed, "Divorce can suck the life out of you." In fact, Charlotte said, "The sting of divorce makes you not want to ever think about dating anyone again." Can we get an AMEN?

She continued, "You work to build the dream of you and your spouse enjoying life in retirement, and poof—suddenly you are paying attorney exorbitant fees and divvying up everything from the children's photos and family heirlooms to your hard-earned retirement fund you built together."

In the other piece of luggage, queens carry a history of repeatedly choosing the same wrong man. We've all encountered "the him" **Queen Melinda** is attracted to. He is fine, six-foot-five, cologne so attuned to his natural scent you want to follow him around the room. Then bam, you're singing the same tune; tired of the drama, the arguing, the cheating, the narcissistic ways. This is the type of man, and relationship, that revisits her life over and over. Melinda says that these men would be such gentlemen and accommodating initially. Elegant dinners and trips to Greece, Paris, and the Maldives on private jets. They would buy her the world if she asked. But like clockwork, as soon as she committed to the relationship, things would drastically change. She'd awaken at different phases of the relationship to see the same man as he authentically was—very controlling and self-absorbed. It became all about where they wanted or did not want to go or how important they were. Different shades on the melanin color chart but displaying the same toxic characteristics: lack of trust, lack of faithfulness, all take no give, and passive-aggressive behaviors. These were just the tip of the iceberg. Melinda would stay in these relationships from three months to two years because she was just too tired to start the process of dating over again. She preferred to stay and enjoy some of the benefits of those relationships than to leave.

Queen Nancy, the life coach, helping others get their life together, married for 15 years and the mother of three children. Her marriage was built on emotional abuse. She gained about 40 pounds over the years and became the target of frequent derogatory comments relating to her weight. She was told constantly no one would want her because she was too fat. Her self-esteem was stomped and trampled on until she finally found the strength to leave. Her self-worth was down. Determined never to allow anyone to devalue her again, she remained alone for eight years and focused on her business. Dating attempts were sporadic and would fizzle when she was spooked by something a potential partner would say that would be reminiscent of her marriage.

Three queens, all beautiful, all intelligent, but nonetheless struggling to keep their crowns erect. The thought of starting over seemed too daunting a task for each of them to take on.

Queens often set their relationship standards high. However, the bar is raised significantly higher after previous hurt. Finding love that meets every prong on your he-must-have list is a challenge I absolutely feel you on. My standards for a prospective boo were so long until a friend of mine said they were exhausting. My reply, "Damn Skippy! If I were to ever marry again, and I am not, he would have to be sent from above, be a Christian who goes to church, have a fierce body (because I work hard to keep myself up), be great in bed and would have to have a whole battery of STD screenings and show me the results!"

But that is not it! He would have to love to travel, and I mean really love to travel, not just faking it until he got into the relationship. He would have to love to dance and be just as tired of dealing with relationship shenanigans as I was. He would have to be spontaneous and love to laugh, and the list went on and on—like 50 items long. And I was serious. No one would have qualified!

Like most queens, my list was a means of keeping me from being deceived or experiencing a broken heart again. Therefore, the conscious mind forces you to believe being single forever is better. And many entrepreneurial queens will bury themselves in work, claiming to want love, but not shifting toward what they want. They hid behind vulnerability and self-limiting beliefs. Some queens grab hold to the fallacy that there are no more good men; the thought of working through or adding one more thing to their schedule, well, is too much to deal with. Truth be told, we were not made to be alone. We were made to have a helpmate, a partner, a husband or companion; we are social beings, and we need each other. But it takes lots of work. Charlotte, Melinda, and Nancy had to clear the emotional clutter that left them believing true love could not be found. Queen Charlotte reclaimed her life after working through the resentment she had for her ex-husband. She realized she had to not only forgive the hurts she experienced but also forgive herself. Forgive herself for what she felt she failed to see early in the relationship that would have prevented her from marrying a man whose goals did not match hers. Queen Charlotte set new standards, reclaimed her life, and gained a genuinely enjoyable relationship with a new boo. Queen Nancy discovered she had characteristics that attracted narcissistic men to her. Although confident in her business, she was very insecure when it came to romantic relationships, and she had critically low-self-esteem. Her partners took advantage of her. They intentionally showered her with those things they knew she desired and would keep her submissive and available. She also tended to immediately smother the men she dated with so much attention that she would neglect her own needs, especially her health. She also didn't hold them accountable for any challenges that may arise, accepting blame herself for any conflicts in the relationships. After recognizing the signs of toxic relationships, such as her needs being neglected and disrespected, constant arguing, and allowing him to be the proverbial bad guy and fall guy when things went awry. After recognizing the signs of toxicity and being intentional about refusing to allow them in her life, this queen found a new companion not cut from the same tainted fabric.

Queen Melinda realized through her work that her weight, although a problem for her, was not a deterrent to dating. She rebuilt her self-esteem, is living a healthier lifestyle by choice (minus the stress of abuse), and has a partner that makes her feel like the queen she is.

No matter your profession, there is always room to be in a loving relationship if you want one. But you must be willing to do the work of clearing the emotional clutter left from previous relationships. Take the time to learn to love yourself first, acknowledge your sabotaging relationship traits, and understand what a sincere productive relationship looks like. You should do this even if you are not ready to date. The first and most important step in this process requires scheduling time for yourself and a space for doing the work. You cannot do the work if you do not commit to penciling yourself in on your schedule. Commit to giving YOU one hour a day in the early morning, on a lunch break, or before bed. The location can be in the quiet of your office, or the office of a counselor, or during a walk on the beach. Commit to investing the time to allow yourself to learn and prepare for love like you commit to your business, your kids, or other priorities. Like doing a deep dive into reflective journaling which allows you to identify trends; examine your fears, desires, and inner thoughts; and helps you to hone in on future expectations or goals. This is more successfully accomplished with a mentor or counselor because it allows you to move through the process without getting stuck or being stopped by intimidation or uncertainty.

So that I don't leave you in the dark about me, it took me six years to work through my baggage and take my life back. For me, the tasks were daunting. At any given moment, any number of emotions would show up. There would be happiness one minute, then I could take a few breaths and be angry as hell and spewing unrecognizable words. And I did this all while going through graduate school, a hurricane, and the death of two parents (to add insult to injury). But in doing so, I managed to work through the disappointment, resentment, and the anger of spending 21 years in a marriage that failed.

The realization I came to through my work was, I was exactly where I was supposed to be at that time. The marriage was not a relationship built on a well-thought-out foundation, and my season in it was over, but my life was not. You see, every relationship has its season, its beginning and expiration dates. Some last a lifetime, and you grow through the ebbs and flows meant to strengthen the foundation. Others start with a bang, bringing you much joy, but only last until the lesson you were meant to learn has been completed. (Or, until someone jumps ship in response to a short- or long-term crisis.) Every relationship situation is meant to activate growth or teach you a valuable life lesson. They become tools in your arsenal of things to do or not to do as you grow as a person.

My work consisted of journaling as a means of releasing all the hurt, anger, and resentment. In doing so, I found out who I really am after that season of marriage was over. I not only set new standards but eventually shortened that list of perfections that would have prevented anyone from entering my personal space. I meditated to gain insight and to keep me grounded. I worked out like crazy, hitting the gym for a circuit training class at five every morning. That extra time in the morning working on me made me feel like a new woman. Since I loved to dance, I reconnected with friends who do as well and learned how to swing-out. Having a healthy tribe of close friends (or a friend) you can confide in, have a glass of wine with, and vent to is especially important to the healing process. True friends will have your best interest at heart and will quickly tell you all the things they knew about your previous failed relationship that they noticed but had to let you work through on your own. Veer away from friends who specialize in excessive negative talk and engage in male-bashing. They will keep you from moving forward in your healing work and leave you stuck in resentment. I know for a while I had the angry black woman look when arrogant men or those who were with a partner looked in my direction in a flirtatious way. I knew I was healed when seemingly respectable men began coming at me like bees to honey, even though I still was not interested in dating. When you are happy and self-assured, you will attract who is wanting what you are putting out. Everything in your life seems to begin to go your way.

My career took off, and I felt damn good! In the process of healing, I reconnected with a former classmate who had a lot of the qualities I listed and thought no man would be able to possess. He matched most of the qualities of a man that I said I wanted on my list. And the things he didn't have or like to do really did not matter because I realized (through my process of healing) I was not perfect either. We both are enjoying a beautiful non-perfect relationship that serves us both well.

So, what is the moral of this story? There are enough good men to go around. Trouble does not have to last always. If you do the work, and you really want to add a loving, authentic, trusting, mutually monogamous relationship to your resume, it will happen. Learn that you do not have to settle. Invest in healing yourself like you would remedy a business problem. Get educated, liberated, and motivated through counseling or a good relationship coach. A relationship coach or mentor will help you to clear self-limiting beliefs that may be sabotaging your efforts to have a successful relationship, help you heal past relationship wounds, and learn to deflect triggers that may come up as you begin dating again. Get help clearing the clutter, setting new standards, learning how to dodge the influence of those who do not have the qualities you desire or don't have your best interest at heart. Do the work, Queen, and get Your Life back! You deserve it.

I would love to have a conversation with you and support you in your efforts to heal and love again. Connect with me at www.safedatingover50.com. Get a complimentary break-through consultation or invite me to talk to your women's group.

ABOUT THE AUTHOR

Cheryl D. Guidry MSN, WHNP-BC, C.P.C. has dedicated her entire professional life to being a women's health advocate both socially and professionally for over 35 years, yet she is still in the business of transforming lives, whether it is related to their physical health or as they struggle to find quality relationships. Cheryl is one relationship coach whose focus is on relationships of single women over 50. She employs patience and experience to quickly identify problems and come up with solutions that change lives. She is a Board-Certified Woman's Health Nurse Practitioner, Certified Professional Life Coach and engages wholly in women empowerment. When you come across her, you have found someone who can listen to you and embrace your uniqueness. A coach with many admirable qualities, she's creative, inspiring, innovative, and a true definition of a pacesetter. Over the years, Cheryl has excelled in passionate coaching and health consulting and relies on her gained experience and practical knowledge to guide her clients. In her work, especially with women, she educates women on reproductive health, sure ways to maintain healthy relationships, and becoming more confident about themselves. She believes that women deserve better lives, and for this reason, she has remained on the vanguard of this struggle. Cheryl's style is grounded in her knowledge, real-life experience, love, ability to understand people, and practical knowledge. With longevity in her field, she possesses an excellent mastery of skills and knowledge that can help women transcend their life challenges. More to her vital works, she focuses immensely on inspiring, encouraging, and empowering women to channel their innate power and maximize their potentials. Cheryl remains grateful for the opportunity to work with these beautiful women. Hopefully, she will continue to be an example, leader, friend, and source of upliftment for them.

Feel free to stay connected with Cheryl Guidry on social media at:

http://safedatingover50.com
Cheryl@safedatingover50.com

PEACE FOR PURPOSE

By

Sylvia Smith Johnson

There was that famous line in the movie "Mahogany" when Brian (Billy Dee Williams) asked Traci (Diana Ross), "What is success without someone you love to share it with?" Oh yes, it was so profound for that moment in the movie. We all screamed because the idea of sharing that success with someone as smooth as Billy Dee Williams seemed like heaven. But coming back to reality, a lot of people will have success and be satisfied with their success without having a "romantic partner" to share it with. After all, that is what he was speaking of. But you can share your success with your family and friends and even strangers, and this could very well bring you great satisfaction. But in reality, the important question is: what good is success when you don't have peace? What good is it to achieve goals and don't have peace of mind to really flow with it? What good is it to make a lot of money, get awards and even prestige, yet you wore yourself out with worry and frustrations. I know too many people who really believe that achieving their dreams and goals will help them achieve a sense of peace they need. They will be able to sleep and rest once they make their move and can see the fruit of their labor. They will be able to stop worrying when "it" all falls into place, and everything will be good … But in all honesty, that is not reality. Let's be for real, rarely will there be a time in life when there are no concerns, especially when you have a business. Your business will bring on many cares when you really care about your service or product and your clients.

I have had a small side business since I got out of college almost 40 years ago. I have been fully self-employed for the last 18 years. And I have had to learn how to operate in a state of peace while juggling life and business. Starting and having your own business is rewarding and stressful at the same time. It is rewarding because you are now doing something that you have chosen to do in order to take control of your own life and making things happen. You could be pursuing a lifelong dream or have found yourself in a position where you need to have income and aren't waiting around until someone hires you. And now, who is the boss? You are the boss!! This is such a power move. Not as in having one up on anyone else but by not leaving your fate in the hands of someone else. After all, no matter how hard you work for others, giving your all, blood, sweat, and tears for another organization; it does not always guarantee you promotion, sufficient income, and recognition for your efforts. Having the power to create a working environment for you and your employees in which you and they would like to work is awesome. You can make sure that you have favorable working conditions that promote success. And you get to set your own hours. You can go on vacation when you choose, and you don't have to ask for permission to get off when you don't feel well or your child or loved one is ill. And in this age of technology, you are never out of reach of your clientele if you choose not to be. So, making that step into self-employment should is exhilarating.

Yet, on the other hand, it can be scary. For now, you are venturing into the world of the unknown. When we are employees, we at least have a little security in that if we do a good job, and the company is stable, the probability of getting paid is pretty high. Not so with a startup, and depending on the industry you are taking the leap into, unpredictable is probably an understatement. You will need to have the funds to pay your bills and your employees if you have them. And unless you have really prepared for this leap, you probably don't have a big stash of cash to sustain you until the income flow is sufficient and steady. This is undoubtedly a major stress factor in entrepreneurship. You are at the mercy of clients, the environment, the government, taxes, donors, supply, demand, and the list goes on. Then you must make sure that you provide quality services and products in order to compete and get people to purchase your product. And oftentimes, those things can send you into a tailspin if you are not very careful. Now don't put the book down here and go back to Egypt.

But back to my original question: What is success if you

don't have peace? Why is having peace so important for an entrepreneur? Isn't stress a great motivator? Answering the last one first, yes, some stress can be a great motivator. It can put pressure on you to do what you know you should be doing. But too much stress can send you into an anxiety-ridden state of paralysis. It can make the problem appear bigger than it is and the solution seem out of reach. It can make you regret ever having taken the chance or opportunity to venture out on your own, causing you to retreat to the perceived safety of "employee" status. Then you would never know what you missed or who missed out because you did not offer your product or service.

Will there ever be a time in entrepreneur land when there is peace? Will there be a time when there are no concerns, no uncertainties, no doubts, questions, or fears? Hopefully, maybe, but probably not, sorry to say. At least one or two of these will be present at all times. Having had my own business for many years now, I wish I could say I have experienced at least one time when I did not have to confront at least one of these peace stealers. And being a certified public accountant, whose clientele consisted mostly of small business owners, I can say that rarely did they experience days without concerns, uncertainties, doubts, questions, or fears. After all, if nothing else raises the stress level, realizing that you are responsible for all of your taxes—and the more money you make, the more taxes you pay—usually sends you into cold sweats. And even worse, even if you don't make a lot of money, you still have to pay taxes. Well, surely, it sounds like I am trying to discourage you from taking the plunge, but on the contrary, I think this is the best decision you can make if you believe this is what you should be doing. You have been given an idea or talent or mission that I believe is part of your divine purpose for this time in your life. So, by all means, go for it and do it and make a difference or impact because that's what makes us part of the cycle of life. Be a supplier, not just a consumer.

Now, if I am not talking about the type of peace when everything is just perfect, the skies are blue, the birds are singing, the bank account is overflowing, everyone is happy and singing and dancing and laughing and whatever that kind of peace looks like to you, what am I talking about? I am speaking of the peace you have when everything is just the opposite. That peace you have when you don't have enough money to pay your expenses. That peace that comes when you owe taxes, but you already spent the government's share. That peace that comes when it seems no one can afford your services, or your overhead is higher than your income. That peace that comes when life happens, and you are trying to run a business and handle your personal circumstances. That peace that comes when you are wondering why you ever decided to do this business. Life is always happening around us. You never know what the next moment will bring. But good or bad, so often we lose our internal peace compass by trying to control what we can't, or even worse, we play out the pending doom in our heads and react accordingly. Again, I am not trying to put fear into your endeavors, but just the opposite. There is a well-known poem, ***Don't Quit*** by John Greenleaf Whittier. This poem, in a nutshell, says when everything seems wrong, rest, but don't quit. Well, I am saying that the way to keep your wits about you and not quit is to keep your peace in the midst of the storm. I want to offer you some suggestions on how to find and keep your peace, staying focused, and riding the wave while turning your business into all that it can be.

First, recognize your limits. Know what you can do in your business and cannot do. You cannot be all in all for everyone. This is something I had to realize being in business for myself. I cannot do everything for everybody. You are only human, and people will put unreasonable demands on your time, talent, and product if you allow them to. Understanding what you do and don't do, can and can't do will help keep you in peace. If you are a caregiver, and you prefer to work with senior citizens, and you know you don't have the stamina to care for children, be careful to not let yourself be put into a situation you know would not be good for you just for the money. This is the best way to end up with a bad reputation when, really, you were just out of your area of expertise. Do a self-analysis so you know who you are and what your strengths are. Doing this will aid you in being your best for your clientele with the confidence and quality necessary to be effective. Nothing can steal our peace more than biting off more than we can chew and stressing ourselves out because we are in over our heads. Know when to refer services to others. You will be less stressed and appreciated for not trying to provide that which you cannot with pride.

This is a big one. Resist worrying over past mistakes and future failures. So many sit around pining over what went wrong and beating themselves up for not doing something a certain way. Well, you know what? You can't undo it. Worrying is not going to change the fact that it happened, and you won't wake up tomorrow with a chance for a do-over. Breathe and start doing damage control. When this storm starts raging, whether in your mind, or real because your mistake had tangible consequences, find your peace in realizing that stressing won't change anything, but actions can fix or at least start the mending process. We so often get bogged down with regrets that we can't move forward. Remind yourself that everyone makes mistakes; no one does everything perfectly all the time. Do not require you to be superhuman, and don't let others condemn you for not being perfect. You aren't and never will be, so that is an unnecessary expectation to put on yourself. Know how to say you are sorry for the mistake and do what you can to right the wrong. Then don't imagine all the things that could go wrong or not work out and get yourself tense fretting over a future event that may or may not happen. Do your best and give yourself some slack for being human. I am not saying give yourself an excuse to provide substandard services or products; just do your best and see what happens. Everything is a process. And we live and learn as we experience.

I like this one best when finding my peace. Take a moment to just be grateful. Be grateful for the opportunity to do what you do. Be grateful for your talent and opportunity. Be grateful for those that have helped you along the way. Be grateful that you are able to serve society in the way that you do. Just start counting your blessings. I have heard too many people who were discouraged say, "What is there to be grateful for?" This mentality will put you in a super chaotic state which will be hard to escape. But if you do find yourself thinking anything like that, I suggest you start digging your way back to peace by finding things, however small, to be thankful for. If you can have those thoughts, that means you have a mind and can still think, and that is something to be thankful for. Be thankful you can see if your eyes work. If you can wiggle your toes, be thankful for that. Just start with the simple, seemingly obvious things, and you will find your list can soon become very long, and your attitude will start to change. You will then start to realize that things can and will probably get better. I believe if you practice being grateful every day, you will find it hard to get to the point of not seeing anything to be grateful for. And it is difficult to be fretful when you are grateful. Try it!

Next thing, rest, take a break, relax your mind, and step away for a period. That could be 10 minutes or 10 days. Get mental and physical rest. Burning the candle at both ends will soon burn you out, and you won't be worth anything to anyone. You will have done yourself, your family, and your clients an injustice. Our bodies and mind were not designed to go without rest. When you find you can't think straight, are easily irritated or frustrated, check out your rest regimen. Find a way to fit it in and get it in. Your peace depends on it. Resting replenishes your mind, body, and spirit. Entrepreneurs are notorious for being workaholics. When you have a 9 to 5, you get to go home. But a self-employed business owner seems to work all the time, and you must make a special effort to cut it off. Remind yourself that "it" will be there tomorrow. And if you are no longer physically able to perform or supply, your clientele will replace you. And if you are sick or dead, they will say "So sorry" and still find someone else to provide the service or product. (I am talking to myself right now. I must remind myself of this at least once a week.)

Last, but definitely not least, see your endeavor as your purpose for this season of your life. Recognize that you did not just come up with the idea all by yourself. This is a big world, and every business is to provide for its inhabitants. Whether food, shelter, care, or even entertainment, these things are for the betterment of society. Give credit that the vision was divinely inspired and the talent necessary to carry out your business, though you may have nurtured and developed it, was already in you. This takes away some of the stress of having to be totally responsible for every aspect of your business, especially the parts that you have no control over. Know that you are not alone and that our creator is not asking or compelling you to do what you cannot do.

When you really understand this, you will start resting and experiencing peace that others will not understand. Let's say you are starting a coaching business. Well, something inside of you tells you that you have the ability to inspire, encourage, and assist people in some areas of their life. Now you have this talent, but you have no idea to whom exactly you will impart your wisdom. And to be honest, it isn't your business. This is where you find peace in knowing that you are part of a bigger plan, and you do your part to be ready when the people start requesting your product. Kind of the "if you build it, they will come" concept. And believe they will come at just the right time.

These are just a few things to remember when doing your business and staying in a peaceful state of mind at the same time. It is very doable and most rewarding. So, whether you are just beginning your adventure into entrepreneurship or are well into your journey, just remember to stay in peace. Embrace this as your God-given purpose to serve His world; know your limits and strengths. Do not worry; get some rest and be grateful. Remember that you will be able to handle the concerns that come your way and even navigate the storms that develop when your mind is clear and calm. You will be able to discern what you can do and what you cannot do, what you have control over and what you do not. You will be able to then act and do what you can and, just as with any situation of life, stop trying to do that which you cannot and let the chips fall as they may and repeat the cycle. Remember, worrying has never fixed or changed one thing for the better but has caused some anxiety and heart attacks and some strokes. Just keep it real. You have everything you need inside of you to be successful; just stay at peace so you can enjoy the journey.

ABOUT THE AUTHOR

 Sylvia Smith Johnson, a Certified Public Accountant, has worked in the field of auditing, accounting, and taxes for over 35 years. Sylvia received her bachelor's degree in accounting from The University of Tennessee, Knoxville. She has been the owner and president of Sylvia Johnson CPA, a full-service firm, for the last 16 years. Her company focuses on providing services to small businesses and nonprofit organizations that are not in need of full-time accounting staff. She is now directing some of her time to share the wisdom she has gained through life experiences by writing, speaking, blogging, and coaching as she helps others realize the importance of peace and experience peace especially when nothing around them is peaceful. She was born in Memphis, TN; moved to Atlanta, GA, as a teen. She has lived in Nashville, TN, since 1992 and has one daughter who also is a graduate of UTK.

Feel free to stay connected with Sylvia Smith Johnson on social media at:

https://www.facebook.com/sylvia.s.johnson.1
sylviajohnsoncpa@gmail.com

TIME GREW MY SERVANT HEART

By

Dr. Aikyna Finch

Time goes by so slowly, and time can do so much, as the song says. Since I was 5 years old, I knew that I was going to be a teacher. I walked into my kindergarten class and saw the ideal example of a teacher for me. I watched this woman empower little children that got negative attention, if any, at home and made them strive for greater. That was my first example of empowerment. That made me want to empower others. As the years went by, my path was changed a little bit, but eventually, I became the teacher that I always knew that I would be.

I worked with K-12 and higher education students throughout my career, but the one thing that all of them needed was encouragement and empowerment. Sometimes I had to fight for them when they had no fight left; sometimes I had to stand for them when they had no strength left. But in the end, most were successful. To watch them walk across the stage, so proud of their achievements and all the hard work that they had done to make it to where they were at that moment, was priceless. That's when I realized that I have a heart for service, a heart for empowerment, a heart for uplifting.

Eventually, in 2016, I had to choose between my service and higher ed administration. I couldn't be the empowering individual that I was called to be and be in that type of atmosphere, so that's when coaching became my Center Stage. As a coach, you lead people toward their aha moment, which in turn empowers them to make the decisions they need to make in their lives. Luckily, two years before, I had taken a coach certification course, and I could go right into my business. This is going to be a true test, and if I could be a businesswoman and stealing power people at the same time, this is a really tough space for servant leaders. It is one thing to serve from your heart, but it's another thing to serve and then charge for it. This became very difficult because bills needed to be paid, but how do you charge for something you do naturally?

So, during this time, while working for what I now call the silent investor, I was embarking on the wonderful world of live streaming. By this time, I had a successful past the cast regular interviews and had spoken as a live streaming expert for the largest live streaming conference at that time. So, I had built a pretty decent following for myself, so it made sense for me to start a business. Up to that point, I was doing live streams on social media and motivation. I also had a podcast that I co-hosted on motivation and women empowerment. I also had a company that I had developed on paper because I had anticipated this moment coming. So, I had all of the pieces to make a successful business, but I just needed the blueprint and the drive to make it happen because, as a servant leader, I have been doing all of these things as a hobby because the silent investor paid the bills, but now the silent investor was gone, it was time for me to use my coaching skills and abilities to make my way in the world.

So, I eventually moved to a new silent investor with more flexibility and more appreciation for my gifts in coaching. This was a win-win because I was able to develop my skills as a coach and my skills as an educator while still being able to work on my business, which became Finch and Associates LLC. This was a place where I could coach, train, speak, and write books about social media, motivation, coaching, technology, everything that I was interested in. I know when you read that sentence, it seems like a whole lot of different things, but each one of them is a facet of me. As a servant leader, when you work very hard to gain a skill set, you don't throw it away; you just build upon it when you have a new focus, and because I was like a sponge when it came to learning things, my passions all merged fairly quickly once I had a business of my own and no outside boundaries to hold me back. Well, here I was with this business that I needed to do something with. I was not interested in having an expensive hobby. I wanted a successful business. 2016 was a very interesting year, and it led into 2017, where the floodgates opened in my favor.

In 2017, many things happened. This was when I started going to conferences and doing social media and correspondence. This was when I started realizing the power of my opinions. I realized that people could see different things that they could do that they never dreamed of by watching my live stream and listening to my commentaries. Many people were choosing what conference to go to the next year. Because of my live streams, people were finding out more about social media and the way that they get to enhance their business from my live streams; it was amazing. It was so exciting to do interviews with different celebrities and influencers while letting people know what was going on in the community. I would always end each event that I went to with a commentary video. I didn't want them to just understand the information from a perception point of view; I wanted them to understand it from an elevation point of view.

One of the events I went to was Collision, an event hosted in New Orleans that is part of a worldwide conference series. Being in that atmosphere opened my eyes to so many different things that my community was not doing. I had a coaching community, and I had a Tech Community, and Collision was definitely part of the startup Tech Community. And by going to that conference, I opened up the possibilities of what could be done to my coaching Community with their businesses. I also took a photo of one of the startup companies, and it was featured in a national publication blog, and that was amazing.

This was also the time when the motivation station radio show was in full effect. It was a very fun project that I did with my co-host Vanessa Canteberry, and it really opened up people's thoughts to motivation. We were already doing the Motivate Social Podcast, but someone came to us and offered us a show on their network, and so we decided to call it motivation station, and it was a way to reach different audiences from what we were reaching in on our podcast, a more faith-based audience. We were reaching 23 countries on that show, and we actually had some pretty good ratings. It was fun, informative, and real. We brought on a lot of different guests that footed that bill as well. That year, the Motivation Station Radio Show was a sponsor for one of the conferences that I did social media for, and the recording and coverage was a big hit in the faith-based community. In December of that year, we decided to end the motivation station show after 1 year.

In 2018, coaching really picked up for me. I co-founded a social media membership site that I still run today. I also started coaching in a program that was developed by my University, and I was certified in coaching by the International Coach Federation (ICF). I also joined the Tennessee chapter and became the social media manager after being referred by one of my friends. I was certified in 2014 by Coach Training Alliance, but getting my ACC from ICF made it truly real. At this point, I was touching the lives of many people, and I was loving every minute of it. Nothing was better than working with clients and helping them reach their greater. I was also training coaches as well. It was a great feeling to share the love of coaching with others who wanted to make a difference as much as I did. This was when I realized the power and gift of coaching. With each coaching class I taught, I saw the light bulbs come on about the importance of coaching and the difference that they were about to make for their future clients and mentees. The energy that they were giving in class fueled me to give them my best.

This was also when I founded the Social Power Summit, a two-day conference that featured women in Tech and people of color in social media that were not getting the opportunities or exposure that they deserved for the brilliance that they were presenting. This was going to prove to be an uphill battle. I learned the dynamic of support and influence. It is one thing to want to change the world, but that really doesn't matter to a group of people that just want to be seen.

To date, I never really paid attention to the type of audience that I had versus the type of person that I was. What do I mean by that? There will come a time when you realize the type of presenter you are versus the type of audience you attract. For example, I am a thought leader, but I talked about social media, so I attracted people who wanted to be seen versus people that wanted to change the world. This became evident when I decided to do my social media conference.

My conference was about the awareness, support, and diversity of social media. This was not flashy enough to people that just wanted to be seen, and they didn't come. The people that were in the room, for the most part, were thought leaders like myself that wanted to learn how to make a difference with their social media and reach the audience that has been waiting on their gifts. It was amazing to have a room full of empowerpreneurs working toward their greater together. There were so many alliances and friendships that were formed at that conference, and I am honored by that, but there were some revelations that were had there as well that led to the end of some alliances and friendships as well. That is what happens when you build events that cause breakthroughs.

People have to come to terms with where they are and their willingness to elevate. I was so proud of my speakers, audiences, and vendors for showing up. Showing up is half the battle, and executing is the other half. If I would have given up on this conference the hundreds of times that I thought about it, then I would not have shown my audience the importance of showing up even when people don't believe in the vision. Because of that conference, I saw people get breakthroughs in their businesses, their purpose, their brands, and their stories. I love looking down my timelines and seeing the people that came to the conference winning using the tips and tools that the speakers shared with them. That is the joy of a thought leader—to see the teachings and purpose working for others!

2019 was the beginning of the shift between my professional and personal life. I started seeing the world from a different lens. Before this point, I thought I could save the world. I thought that all I had to do was put it out there, and it was so. I had to realize my shortcomings for what they were. Sometimes you have to do a reinvention of your life. Sometimes you will look around, and you will not recognize where you are and who you have become. It was my job to truly have a self-reflection moment. When I came out of the self-reflection moment, I saw who I was, where I was, but then I visualized who and where I wanted to be and decided to make it a reality. I made a plan for the year of all the professional and personal things I wanted to do with my life, and the transformation began. Out of the 11 professional things I wanted to do, I got eight done, and out of the five personal things I wanted to do, I got four things done.

So, why does this matter? It matters because even the person that inspires everyone has to eventually start empowering themselves. In order for me to keep being the beacon of hope and light that I wanted to be for others, I had to start being there for myself. I had to start cleaning up my mind, body, and spirit. I had to let go of all the things that were holding me back. I either had to fix them, release them, or accept them, but they could no longer be a hindrance in my life.

In my business, there were some things that I really didn't like to do as a business owner, and in this year of exploration and transformation, I learned how to do these things. With each success and failure, the one thing I could say is that at least, I tried, and that's a lot more than I can have said in the years past. I had a tendency to shy away from things that didn't come easily and naturally to me because so many things did, so there was no need to waste time on things that didn't. But there comes a time when you have to realize that everything is not going to come naturally to you, and it's still necessary. It wasn't easy; it wasn't fun, but it was growth.

When you invest in yourself so that you can improve the lives of others, it is a noble thing. It is something that thought leaders do all the time, but it is hardly ever acknowledged. Remember that the journey done in the background is much more fulfilling than the ones done in the spotlight. There will be people that never acknowledge your part in their success, and that is okay. Then there will be people that will never be able to thank you enough. The point is that if you are looking for praise for everything you do, you need to stop now because it will never happen as an empowerpreneur. What will happen is that you will continue to empower, educate, and motivate your tribe because you are purposed to make the world a better place in your space of expertise.

At the end of the day, everyone will not like, want, love, respect, or need you ... Stop looking for it! That will save you a lot of heartache that you don't need and energy that they don't deserve!!! People will try to stop you from reaching your potential because they can't see their own. You owe it to yourself and the people that are waiting on your greatness to keep pushing forward.

Focus on the people and things that do like, want, love, respect, or need you because they deserve your time and energy. They will be there during your life, lifting you up and supporting you along the way! If the people in my life that served as catalysts for my greatness would have given up, where would I be now? This is the question I ask myself every time I think about giving up on my calling. I remember that I am not for everybody, but I am for somebody, and that somebody may still be searching for me.

ABOUT THE COMPILER

Dr. Aikyna Finch is a podcaster, social media coach, and speaker. She coaches in the areas of Empowerment, Life, and Social Media at the individual and group levels from her company Finch and Associates LLC. She is the co-host of the Motivate Social Podcast broadcast by her company Changing Minds Online. She speaks and livestreams on the topics of Motivation, Education, and Social Media. In 2018, she founded the Social Power Summit, an event with a live and virtual component for women in STEM and people of color in social media to have a platform where they can shine.

Dr. Finch is the co-author of six books and launched her first solo project, Motivation Ignited, in November of 2016. She is a contributor for Huffington Post, Goalcast, Forbes, and Thrive Global. She has been interviewed and featured on Huffington Post, Hello Beautiful, Women Speakers Association, and many others. She has spoken on many platforms, including Periscope Summit, Women In Leadership Summit and many more! She can be found on all Social Media Platforms at DrADFinch.

Dr. Finch is an educator. She received a Doctorate of Management, an MBA in Technology Management, and an

Executive MBA from Colorado Technical University. She has an MS in Management in Marketing and an MS in Information Systems in IT Project Management from Strayer University and a BS in Aeronautical Technology in Industrial Electronics from the School of Engineering of Tennessee State University. She is a former Campus and Faculty Dean, her teaching disciplines, including business, marketing, social media, and information systems at the graduate and undergraduate levels. She has published and presented on topics related to youth and adult education, social media, and job search.

Feel free to stay connected with Dr. Aikyna Finch on social media at:

http://aikynafinch.com
http://socialpowersummit.com
http://changingmindsonline.com

ACKNOWLEDGMENTS

To every author and supporter that made this book possible; thank you so much for believing in the vision of this book and the series as a whole. This would not have happened without you.

I would like to express a special thank you to Vanessa Canteberry of Inspired By Vanessa for serving as the book consultant for this anthology.

Sincerely,
Dr. Aikyna Finch

www.ingramcontent.com/pod-product-compliance
Lightning Source LLC
Chambersburg PA
CBHW051459050726
47593CB00005B/2139